Threatening Communications and Behavior

PERSPECTIVES ON THE PURSUIT OF PUBLIC FIGURES

Cherie Chauvin, *Editor*

Board on Behavioral, Cognitive, and Sensory Sciences

Division of Behavioral and Social Sciences and Education

NATIONAL RESEARCH COUNCIL
OF THE NATIONAL ACADEMIES

THE NATIONAL ACADEMIES PRESS
Washington, D.C.
www.nap.edu

THE NATIONAL ACADEMIES PRESS   500 Fifth Street, N.W.   Washington, DC 20001

NOTICE: The project that is the subject of this report was approved by the Governing Board of the National Research Council, whose members are drawn from the councils of the National Academy of Sciences, the National Academy of Engineering, and the Institute of Medicine.

This study was supported by Contract/Grant No. BCS-0827794 between the National Academy of Sciences and the National Science Foundation. Any opinions, findings, conclusions, or recommendations expressed in this publication are those of the author(s) and do not necessarily reflect the views of the organizations or agencies that provided support for the project.

International Standard Book Number-13:   978-0-309-18670-4
International Standard Book Number-10:   0-309-18670-6

Copies of this report are available from National Academies Press, 500 Fifth Street, N.W., Lockbox 285, Washington, DC 20055; (800) 624-6242 or (202) 334-3313 (in the Washington metropolitan area); Internet, http://www.nap.edu.

Copyright 2011 by the National Academy of Sciences. All rights reserved.

Printed in the United States of America.

Suggested citation: National Research Council. (2011). *Threatening Communications and Behavior: Perspectives on the Pursuit of Public Figures.* C. Chauvin, ed. Board on Behavioral, Cognitive, and Sensory Sciences, Division of Behavioral and Social Sciences and Education. Washington, DC: The National Academies Press.

THE NATIONAL ACADEMIES
Advisers to the Nation on Science, Engineering, and Medicine

The **National Academy of Sciences** is a private, nonprofit, self-perpetuating society of distinguished scholars engaged in scientific and engineering research, dedicated to the furtherance of science and technology and to their use for the general welfare. Upon the authority of the charter granted to it by the Congress in 1863, the Academy has a mandate that requires it to advise the federal government on scientific and technical matters. Dr. Ralph J. Cicerone is president of the National Academy of Sciences.

The **National Academy of Engineering** was established in 1964, under the charter of the National Academy of Sciences, as a parallel organization of outstanding engineers. It is autonomous in its administration and in the selection of its members, sharing with the National Academy of Sciences the responsibility for advising the federal government. The National Academy of Engineering also sponsors engineering programs aimed at meeting national needs, encourages education and research, and recognizes the superior achievements of engineers. Dr. Charles M. Vest is president of the National Academy of Engineering.

The **Institute of Medicine** was established in 1970 by the National Academy of Sciences to secure the services of eminent members of appropriate professions in the examination of policy matters pertaining to the health of the public. The Institute acts under the responsibility given to the National Academy of Sciences by its congressional charter to be an adviser to the federal government and, upon its own initiative, to identify issues of medical care, research, and education. Dr. Harvey V. Fineberg is president of the Institute of Medicine.

The **National Research Council** was organized by the National Academy of Sciences in 1916 to associate the broad community of science and technology with the Academy's purposes of furthering knowledge and advising the federal government. Functioning in accordance with general policies determined by the Academy, the Council has become the principal operating agency of both the National Academy of Sciences and the National Academy of Engineering in providing services to the government, the public, and the scientific and engineering communities. The Council is administered jointly by both Academies and the Institute of Medicine. Dr. Ralph J. Cicerone and Dr. Charles M. Vest are chair and vice chair, respectively, of the National Research Council.

www.national-academies.org

BOARD ON BEHAVIORAL, COGNITIVE, AND SENSORY SCIENCES
JANUARY 2011

Philip Rubin (*Chair*), Haskins Laboratories and Yale University
Lisa Feldman Barrett, Department of Psychology, Northeastern University
Linda Bartoshuk, College of Dentistry, University of Florida
Richard J. Bonnie, Institute of Law, Psychiatry and Public Policy, University of Virginia
John Cacioppo, Department of Psychology, University of Chicago
Susan Carey, Department of Psychology, Harvard University
Susan T. Fiske, Department of Psychology, Princeton University
Nina G. Jablonski, Department of Anthropology, Pennsylvania State University
Patricia K. Kuhl, Department of Speech and Hearing Sciences, University of Washington
Jonathan D. Moreno, Departments of Medical Ethics and History and Sociology of Science, University of Pennsylvania
Richard Nisbett, Department of Psychology, University of Michigan
Michael L. Posner, Department of Psychology, University of Oregon (*Emeritus*)
Valerie F. Reyna, Department of Human Development and Psychology, Cornell University
Richard M. Shiffrin, Psychology Department, Indiana University
Brian Wandell, Department of Psychology, Stanford University

Barbara A. Wanchisen, *Director*
Mary Ellen O'Connell, *Deputy Director*
Cherie Chauvin, *Program Officer*
Christie R. Jones, *Program Associate*
Renée L. Wilson Gaines, *Senior Program Assistant*
Matthew D. McDonough, *Senior Program Assistant*

Acknowledgments

The Board on Behavioral, Cognitive, and Sensory Sciences (BBCSS) wishes to thank the National Science Foundation (NSF) for its generous support of BBCSS activities. Without NSF's assistance, this publication would not have been possible. Early drafts of these papers were written to inform a federal agency research agenda, but they were subsequently substantially revised to more broadly review the literature on the correlation between communication-relevant factors and the likelihood that an individual who poses a threat will act on it. The factors considered are computerized text analysis, communication, and forensic psychology: together, they represent a synthesis of current knowledge that may provide ideas for potential new research directions.

Each paper has been reviewed in draft form by individuals chosen for their diverse perspectives and technical expertise, in accordance with procedures approved by the National Research Council's Report Review Committee. The purpose of this independent review is to provide candid and critical comments that will assist the institution in making its publications as sound as possible and to ensure that the papers meet institutional standards for objectivity and evidence. The review comments and draft manuscript remain confidential to protect the integrity of the scientific process.

We thank the following individuals for their review of one or more of the papers in this volume: Nancy Cooke, Department of Applied Psychology, Arizona State University; Robert A. Fein, Department of Psychiatry, McLean Hospital, Harvard Medical School; Jeffrey T. Hancock,

Department of Communication, Cornell University; Eduard Hovy, Information Sciences Institute, University of Southern California; Gary King, Department of Government, Harvard University; Tim Levine, Department of Communication, Michigan State University; Sharon Smith, Federal Bureau of Investigation (retired) and Forensic Psycholinguistics, LLC.

Although the reviewers listed above provided many constructive comments and suggestions, they were not asked to endorse the content of the papers, nor did they see the final draft before publication. The review of this collection of papers was overseen by Linda Waite of the Department of Sociology at the University of Chicago. Appointed by the National Research Council, she was responsible for making certain that an independent examination of the papers was carried out in accordance with institutional procedures and that all review comments were carefully considered. Responsibility for the final content of this publication rests entirely with the authors and the institution.

Contents

Introduction *Philip E. Rubin and Barbara A. Wanchisen*	1
Using Computerized Text Analysis to Assess Threatening Communications and Behavior *Cindy K. Chung and James W. Pennebaker*	3
Communication-Based Research Related to Threats and Ensuing Behavior *H. Dan O'Hair, Daniel Rex Bernard, and Randy R. Roper*	33
Approaching and Attacking Public Figures: A Contemporary Analysis of Communications and Behavior *J. Reid Meloy*	75
Appendix: Biographical Sketches of Contributors	103

Introduction

Philip E. Rubin and Barbara A. Wanchisen

Today's world of rapid social, technological, and behavioral change provides new opportunities for communications with few limitations of time or space. The ease by which communications can be made without personal proximity has dramatically affected the volume, types, and topics of communications between individuals and groups. Through these communications, people leave behind an ever-growing collection of traces of their daily activities, including digital footprints provided by text, voice, and other modes of communication. Many personal communications now take place in public forums, and social groups form between individuals who previously might have acted in isolation. Ideas are shared and behaviors encouraged, including threatening or violent ideas and behaviors. Meanwhile, new techniques for aggregating and evaluating diverse and multimodal information sources are available to security services that must reliably identify communications indicating a high likelihood of future violence.

In the context of this changed and changing world of communications and behavior, the Board on Behavioral, Cognitive, and Sensory Sciences of the National Research Council presents this volume of three papers as one portion of the vast subject of threatening communications and behavior. We thank the National Science Foundation for funding of the Board, making this special publication possible. The papers review the behavioral and social sciences research on the likelihood that someone who engages in abnormal and/or threatening communications will actually then try to do harm. The focus of the papers is on how scientific knowledge can inform and advance future research on threat assessments, in part by considering the approaches and techniques used to analyze communications and behavior in the dynamic context of today's world.

Each author was asked to present and assess scientific research on the correlation between communication-relevant factors and the likelihood that an individual who poses a threat will act on it. The authors were encouraged to consider not only communications containing direct threats, but also odd and inappropriate communications that could display evidence of fixation, obsession, grandiosity, entitled reciprocity, and mental illness.

In "Using Computerized Text Analysis to Assess Threatening Communications and Behavior," Cindy K. Chung and James W. Pennebaker provide an overview of computerized language techniques for detecting and assessing text-based threats. Approaches include the analysis of language-based datasets (corpora) to help identify and understand threatening communications and responses to them through the study of words.

In "Communications-Based Research Related to Threats and Ensuing Behavior," H. Dan O'Hair, Daniel Rex Bernard, and Randy R. Roper stress the importance and difficulty of using knowledge gained from communication theory and practice to study threatening behavior and develop useful strategies for managing violent behavior.

In "Approaching and Attacking Public Figures: A Contemporary Analysis of Communications and Behavior," J. Reid Meloy reviews and integrates recent research on threatening communication and its relationship to escalation, approach, or attack behaviors toward public figures.

The papers in this collection were written within the context of protecting high-profile public figures from potential attack or harm. The research, however, is broadly applicable to U.S. national security including potential applications for analysis of communications from leaders of hostile nations and public threats from terrorist groups. This work highlights the complex psychology of threatening communications and behavior, and it offers knowledge and perspectives from multiple domains that can contribute to a deeper understanding of the value of communications in predicting and preventing violent behaviors.

Using Computerized Text Analysis to Assess Threatening Communications and Behavior

Cindy K. Chung and James W. Pennebaker

Understanding the psychology of threats requires expertise across multiple domains. Not only must the actions, words, thoughts, emotions, and behaviors of the person making a threat be examined, but the world of the recipient of the threats also needs to be understood. The problem is more complex when considering that threats can be made by individuals or groups and can be directed toward individuals or groups. A threat, then, can occur across any domain and on multiple levels and must be understood within the social context in which it occurs.

Within the field of psychology, most research on threats has focused on the nonverbal correlates of aggression. In the animal literature, for example, considerable attention has been paid to behaviors that signify dominance or submission. Various species of birds, fish, and mammals often change their appearance by becoming larger when threatening others. Dominance and corresponding threat displays have also been found in vocalization, gaze, and even smell signals (e.g., Buss, 2005). In the literature on humans, an impressive number of studies have analyzed threatening behaviors by studying posture, facial expression, tone of voice, and an array of biological changes (Hall et al., 2005).

The authors wish to acknowledge funding from the Army Research Institute (W91WAW-07-C-0029), CIFA (DOD H9c104-07-C-0014), NSF (NSF-NSCC-090482), DIA (HHM-402-10-C-0100), and START (DHS Z934002). They would also like to thank Douglas H. Harris, Cherie Chauvin, and Amanda Schreier for their helpful comments in the preparation of the manuscript.

Although nonverbal features of threats are clearly important, many of the most dangerous threats between people are conveyed using language. Whether among individuals, groups, or entire nations, early threats often involve one or more people using words to warn others. Despite the obvious importance of natural language as the delivery system of threats, very few social scientists have been able to devise simple systems to identify or calibrate language-based threats. Only recently, with the advent of computer technology and the availability of large language-based datasets, have scientists been able to start to identify and understand threatening communications and responses to them through the study of words (Cohn et al., 2001; Pennebaker and Chung, 2005, 2008; Smith, 2004, 2008; Smith et al., 2008).

This paper provides a general overview of computerized language assessment strategies relevant to the detection and assessment of word-based threats. It is important to appreciate that this work is in its infancy. Consequently, there are no agreed-on methods or theories that have defined the field. Indeed, the "field" is currently made up of a small group of laboratories generally working independently with very different backgrounds and research goals. The current review explores threats from a decidedly social-psychological perspective. As such, the emphasis is on the ways in which word use can reveal important features of a threatening message and also the psychological nature of the speaker and the target of the threatening communication.

Whereas traditional language analyses have emphasized the content of a threatening communication (i.e., what the speaker explicitly says), this review focuses on the language style of the message, especially those words that people cannot readily manipulate (for a review, see Chung and Pennebaker, 2007). This is especially helpful in the area of assessing threatening communications and actual behavior because subtle markers of language style (e.g., use of pronouns or articles) can reveal behavioral intent that the speaker may be trying to withhold from the target. Finally, this paper discusses methods that have the goal of automated analyses and largely draws on word count approaches, which are increasingly being used in the social sciences. Computerized tools are especially helpful for establishing a high standard of reliability in any given analysis and for real-time or close to real-time assessment of threatening communications, so that our analyses might one day lead to interventions as opposed to just retrospective case studies.

This paper also briefly describes common automated methods available to study language content and language style. Next, a classification scheme for different types of threats is presented that serves as the organizing principle for this review. The next section summarizes empirical research that has been conducted to assess intent and actual behaviors in contexts of varying stakes using text analysis. The review concludes with a discussion of the gaps where research is desperately needed across various fields, along with our perspective on how to improve predictions and an emphasis on how various models should be built and applied.

TEXT ANALYSIS METHODS

Features of language or word use can be counted and statistically analyzed in multiple ways. The existing approaches can be categorized into three broad methodologies: (1) judge-based thematic content analysis, (2) computerized word pattern analysis, and (3) word count strategies. All are valid approaches to understanding threatening communications and can potentially yield complimentary results to both academic and nonacademic investigators. While it is beyond the scope of this paper to review each approach in detail, an overview is given below. Then the discussion focuses on word count strategies, which serve as the basis for the remainder of the review.

Judge-Based Thematic Content Analysis

Qualitative approaches use an expert or a group of judges to systematically rate particular texts along various themes. Such approaches have explored the subjective or psychological meaning of language within a phrase or sentence (e.g., Semin et al., 1995), conversational turn (e.g., Tannen, 1993), or an entire narrative (e.g., McAdams, 2001). Thematic content analyses have been widely applied for studying a variety of psychological phenomena, such as motive imagery (e.g., Atkinson and McClelland, 1948; Heckhausen, 1963; Winter, 1991), explanatory styles (Peterson, 1992), cognitive complexity (Suedfeld et al., 1992), psychiatric syndromes (Gottschalk et al., 1997), and goal structures (Stein and Albro, 1997).

Several problems exist with qualitative approaches to text analysis. Judge-based coding requires elaborate coding schemes, along with multiple trained raters. The reliability of judges' ratings must be assessed and reevaluated early in the process through extensive discussions. Consideration of time and effort has limited analyses of this kind to small numbers of individuals per analysis. For the analysis of completely open-ended text, for example, when a series of very different threatening communications are assessed for the probability of leading to actual threatening behaviors, the coding schemes developed in judge-based thematic content analysis may not be applicable or particularly relevant to any new threat or document.

As a side note, the authors have spoken with and read about a number of "expert" language analysts who often market their own language analysis methods. Some of these approaches claim to reliably assess deception, author identification, or other intelligence-relevant dimensions. Often, it is claimed that the various methods have accuracy rates of more than 90 to 95 percent. To our knowledge, no human-based judge system has ever been independently assessed by a separate laboratory or been tested outside of experimentally produced and manipulated stimuli. Given the current state of knowledge, it is inconceivable that any language assessment method—whether by human judges or the best computers in the world—could reliably detect real-world deception or other psychological quality at rates greater than 80 percent, even in highly controlled datasets. This issue will be discussed in greater detail later.

Computerized Word Pattern Analysis

Rather than exploring text "top down" within the context of previously defined psychological content dimensions, word pattern strategies mathematically detect "bottom up" how words covary across large samples of text (Foltz, 1996; Poppin, 2000) or the degree to which words overlap within texts (e.g., Graesser et al., 2004). One particularly promising strategy is Latent Semantic Analysis (LSA; see, e.g., Landauer and Dumais, 1997), which is a method used to learn how writing samples are similar to one another based on how words are used together across documents. For example, LSA has been used to detect whether or not a student essay has hit all the major points covered in a textbook or the degree to which a student essay is similar to a group of essays previously graded with top grades on the same topic (e.g., Landauer et al., 1998).

Not only can word pattern analyses detect the similarity of groups of text, they can also be used to extract the underlying topics of text samples (see Steyvers and Griffiths, 2007). One example of a topic modeling approach in the social sciences is the Meaning Extraction Method (MEM; Chung and Pennebaker, 2008). MEM finds clusters of words that tend to co-occur in a corpus. The clusters tend to form coherent themes that have been shown to produce valid dimensions for a variety of corpora. For example, Pennebaker and Chung (2008) found MEM-derived word factors of al-Qaeda statements and interviews that differentially peaked during the times when those topics were most salient to al-Qaeda's missions. MEM-derived factors have been shown to hold content validity across multiple domains. Since the MEM does not require a predefined dictionary (only characters separated by spaces), and translation occurs only at the very end of the process, MEM has served as an unbiased way to examine psychological constructs across multiple languages (e.g., Ramirez-Esparza et al., 2008, in press; Wolf et al., 2010a, 2010b).

Word pattern analyses are generally statistically based and therefore require large corpora to identify reliable word patterns (e.g., Biber et al., 1998). Some word pattern tools feature modules developed from discourse processing, linguistics, and communication theories (e.g., Crawdad Technologies[1]; Graesser et al., 2004), representing a combination of top-down and bottom-up processing capabilities. Overall, word pattern approaches are able to assess high-level features of language to assess commonalities within a large group of texts.

Word Count Strategies

The third general methodology focuses on word count strategies. These strategies are based on the assumption that the words people use convey psychological information over and above their literal meaning and independent of their semantic context. Word count approaches typically rely on a set of dictionaries with precategorized terms. The categories can be grammatical categories (e.g., adverbs, pronouns, prepositions, verbs) or psychological categories (e.g., positive emotions, cognitive words, social words). While grammatical categories are fixed (i.e., entries belong in one or multiple known categories), psychological categories are formed by judges' ratings on whether or not each word belongs in a category. Computerized software can then be programmed to categorize words appearing in text according to the dictionary that it references. Accordingly, these programs typically allow for the use of new, user-defined dictionaries, enabling broader or more specific sampling of word categories.

Today, there is an ever-increasing number of applications of word count analyses in clinical psychology (e.g., Gottschalk, 1997), criminology and forensic psychology (e.g., Adams, 2002, 2004), cultural and cross-language studies (e.g., Tsai et al., 2004), and personality assessments (e.g., Pennebaker and King, 1999; Mehl et al., 2006). An increasingly popular tool used for text analysis in psychology is Linguistic Inquiry and Word Count (LIWC; Pennebaker et al., 2007). LIWC is a computerized word counting tool that searches for approximately 4,000 words and word stems and categorizes them into grammatical (e.g., articles, numbers, pronouns), psychological (e.g., cognitive, emotions, social), or content (e.g., achievement, death, home) categories. Results are reported as a percentage of words in a given text file, indicating the degree to which a particular category was used. The words in LIWC categories have previously been validated by independent judges, and

---

[1]Find Crawdad text analysis software at http://www.crawdadtech.com, Crawdad Technologies LLC [April 2010].

use of the categories within texts has been shown to be a reliable marker for a number of psychologically meaningful constructs (Pennebaker et al., 2003; Tausczik and Pennebaker, 2010).

Using LIWC, word counts have been shown to have modest yet reliable links to personality and demographics. For example, one study across 14,000 texts of varying genres found that women tend to use more personal pronouns and social words than men and that men tend to use more articles, numbers, and fewer verbs (Newman et al., 2008). Together, these findings suggest that women are more socially oriented and that men tend to focus more on objects. Word count tools have effectively uncovered psychological states from spoken language (e.g., Mehl et al., 2006), in published literature (e.g., Pennebaker and Stone, 2003), and in computer-mediated communications (e.g., Chung et al., 2008; Oberlander and Gill, 2006). There is also evidence that word counts are diagnostic of various psychiatric disorders and can reflect specific psychotic symptoms (Junghaenel et al., 2008; Oxman et al., 1982). For example, Junghaenel and colleagues found that psychotic patients tend to use fewer cognitive mechanism and communication words than do people who are not suffering from a mental disorder, reflecting psychotic patients' tendencies to avoid in-depth processing and their general disconnect from social bonds. These studies provide evidence that word use is reflective of thoughts and behaviors that characterize psychological states. Word counts provide meaningful measures for a variety of thoughts and behaviors.

LANGUAGE CONTENT VERSUS LANGUAGE STYLE

Most early content analysis approaches by both humans and computers focused on words related to specific themes. By analyzing an open-ended interview, a human or computer can detect theme-related words such as family, health, illness, and money. Generally, these words are nouns and regular verbs. Nouns and regular verbs are "content heavy" in that they define the primary categories and actions dictated by the speaker or writer. It makes sense; to have a conversation, it is important to know what people are talking about.

However, there is much more to communication than content. Humans are also highly attentive to the ways in which people convey a message. Just as there is linguistic content, there is also linguistic style—how people put their words together to create a message. What accounts for "style"? Consider the ways by which three different people might summarize how they feel about ice cream:

Person A: I'd have to say that I like ice cream.
Person B: The experience of eating a scoop of ice cream is certainly quite satisfactory.
Person C: Yummy. Good stuff.

The three people differ in their use of pronouns, large versus small words, verbosity, and other dimensions. We can begin to detect linguistic style by paying attention to "junk words"—those words that do not convey much in the ways of content (for a review, see Chung and Pennebaker, 2007; Pennebaker et al., 2003). These junk words, usually referred to as function words, serve as the cement that holds the content words together. In English, function words include pronouns (e.g., *I, they, it*), prepositions (e.g., *with, to, for*), articles (e.g., *a, an, the*), conjunctions (e.g., *and, because, or*), auxiliary verbs (e.g., *is, have, will*), and a limited number of other words. Although there are less than 200 common function words, they account for over half of the words used in everyday speech.

Function words are virtually invisible in daily reading and speech. Even most language experts could not tell if the past few paragraphs have used a high or low percentage of pronouns or articles. People are reliable in their use across contexts and over time. Although most everyone uses far more pronouns in informal settings than in formal ones, the highest pronoun use in informal contexts tends to be by the same people who use pronouns at high rates in formal contexts (Pennebaker and King, 1999). Analyzing function words at the paragraph, page, or broader text level completely ignores context. The ultimate difference between the current approach and more traditional linguistic strategies is that function words tell us about the psychology of the writer/speaker rather than what is explicitly being communicated.

Given that function words are so difficult to control, examining the use of these words in natural language samples has provided a nonreactive way to explore social and personality processes. Much like other implicit measures used in experimental laboratory studies in psychology, the authors or speakers examined often are not aware of the dependent variable under investigation (Fazio and Olson, 2003). In fact, most of the language samples from word count studies come from sources in which natural language is recorded for purposes other than linguistic analysis and therefore have the advantage of being more externally valid than the majority of studies involving implicit measures. For this reason, function words are particularly useful in uncovering the relationship between intent and actual behaviors as they occur outside the laboratory.

CLASSIFICATION SCHEME FOR THREATS

One of the difficulties in examining threatening communications and actual behaviors is that researchers typically do not have access to a large group of similar documents on threats and subsequent behaviors. In addition, threats differ tremendously in form, type, and actual intent. Also, situational features across multiple threats cannot be cleanly or confidently classified into discrete categories in order to generalize to new threats. Many of these difficulties in research on threatening communications overlap with the difficulties in research on deception, for which empirical and naturalistic research has made considerable progress through the use of computerized text analyses (for a review, see Hancock et al., 2008).

Comparison with Features of Research on Deception

Deception has been defined as "a successful or [an] unsuccessful deliberate attempt, without forewarning, to create in another a belief . . . the communicator considers . . . untrue" (Vrij, 2000, p. 6; see also Vrij, 2008). This commonly accepted definition of deception notes several features that could be used to succinctly define threatening communications within the task of predicting behaviors (see Table 1-1). Specifically, Vrij's definition includes information about outcome, intent, timing, social features and goals, and a psychological interpretation of the actor. Threatening communications can be compared along all of these features.

A threatening communication will likely carry the language cues used

TABLE 1-1 Comparison of Features in Deceptive Versus Threatening Communications

Features	Deception	Threats
Outcome	Successful/unsuccessful	Fulfilled/unfulfilled
Intent	Deliberate	Deliberate/not deliberate
Timing	Without forewarning	With/without forewarning
Social features/goals	Create belief in another	Communicate possibility of harm/no harm
Psychology of actor	Communicator considers communication to be untrue	Communicator considers threat to be untrue (i.e., has no intent to substantiate the threat) or true (i.e., has real intent to substantiate the threat)

SOURCE: Defining features of deception from Vrij (2000, 2008).

in deception if the communicator knows that the message is false (i.e., has no intent to substantiate the threat). This situation is akin to "bluffing," when a threat is made to achieve some goal(s) by creating in another a belief that the threat is real, when the communicator is aware that it is not. This suggests that, for text analysis of threatening communications, language cues that have reliably been found to signal deception can be used to classify this type of threat as being less likely to be fulfilled. When the communicator knows that the threat is true (i.e., has real intent to substantiate the threat), language cues that have reliably been found to signal honesty can be used to classify this type of threat as being more likely to be fulfilled.

The distinction between deception and threatening communications regarding timing is also an important point. Most language samples of deception come from retrospective accounts of some event. With language samples of threatening communications, often the threatening message is revisited after the act. However, a threat, by definition, is received before the act of harm, and so the language samples analyzed to investigate threats versus deceptive messages typically come from different time points. With some threats there is the possibility of intervention.

These features permit classification of four different types of threats (see Table 1-2). Threats that might have the language features of deception are bluffs and latent threats. Threats that might have the language features

TABLE 1-2 Classification Scheme and Features of Threats

Feature	Type of Threat			
	Real Threat	Bluff	Latent Threat	Nonthreat
Outcome	Fulfilled	Unfulfilled	Fulfilled	N.A.
Intent	Deliberate	Deliberate	Deliberate	Not deliberate
Timing	Forewarning	Forewarning	No forewarning	N.A.
Social features/goals	Communicate harm	Communicate harm	Communicate no harm	Communicate no harm
Psychology of actor	Communicator considers true	Communicator considers untrue	Communicator considers untrue	Communicator considers true
Language features of deception	Honest	Deceptive	Deceptive	Honest

NOTE: N.A. = not available.

of honesty are real threats and nonthreats. Briefly described, a real threat is made known to the target before the harm occurs, with real intent to carry through on the threat. An example would be President George H. W. Bush's threat to Saddam Hussein to leave Kuwait or a coalition attack would follow. In this case, the threat was directly communicated beforehand and was followed by the promised action.

A bluff is a threat that is made known to the target but with no intent to act on the threat. Multiple examples can be found in the speeches of Saddam Hussein, who explicitly stated and implicitly suggested that his army had the capability of inflicting mass casualties on coalition forces prior to both the Persian Gulf War of 1991 and the more recent war beginning in 2003. Latent threats are those that are concealed to the target before the harm occurs, with real intent to carry through on the threat. An example might be the case of Bernard Madoff, who was recently imprisoned for masterminding a Ponzi scheme that bankrupted hundreds of innocent investors. Many people invested their money with Madoff under his guise of a trusted financier. In this case, no threat was communicated, but his communications with victims likely would have shown linguistic markers of deception.

Nonthreats are communications from people who have no intent to harm. Indeed, nonthreats can be considered control communications in the sense that the speaker speaks honestly about events, actions, or intentions that the speaker believes to be nonthreatening.

Nonthreats, like all other forms of threat communication, carry with them another potentially vexing dimension: the role of the listener or target of the communication. Table 1-2 is based on the speaker's intent and behaviors, not the listener's. It is possible that a speaker can issue a true threat but that the listener perceives it as a bluff. By the same token, latent threats and nonthreats can variously be interpreted in both benign and threatening ways. Failure to adequately detect a real threat or to falsely perceive a true nonthreat may say as much about the perceiver as the message itself. For example, Saddam Hussein's apparent failure to appreciate coalition threats in both 1991 and 2003 very likely reflected something about his own ways of seeing the world.

Just as there are likely personality dimensions of people who deny or fail to appreciate real threats, a long tradition in psychology has been interested in the opposite pattern—the belief that a real threat exists when actually one does not. Dozens of examples of this can be seen in American politics, especially among those on the extreme left and right. During the George W. Bush years, many far-left pundits were convinced that the administration was planning to do away with the First Amendment. Currently, many right-wing voices claim that the Obama administration wants to outlaw all guns—resulting in record sales of firearms and ammunition.

From a linguistic perspective it is important that researchers explore the natural language use of both communicators and perceivers. For example, Hancock et al. (2008) have shown linguistics changes on the part of a listener who is being deceived, demonstrating that deception might be better detected and understood by considering the greater social dynamics in which it takes place (see also Burgoon and Buller, 2008, for a review of Interpersonal Deception Theory). Situations are dynamic, and there are possibilities that real threats could be revoked or unsuccessfully attempted or that bluffs might be carried out under pressure. However, the key feature in language analyses is that an attempt is made to understand the psychology or deep-structure processes underlying the threats. In this regard, the personality or psychological states of both speakers and targets can be assessed in order to better understand the nature, probability, and evolving dynamics of a given threat.

REVIEW OF EMPIRICAL RESEARCH ON COMMUNICATED INTENT AND ACTUAL BEHAVIORS USING TEXT ANALYSIS

To distinguish between real threats and bluffs, or between latent threats and nonthreats, the first step is to assess whether or not a given communication is deceptive. To detect deception, computerized text analysis methods have been applied to natural language samples in both experimental laboratory tests and a limited number of real-world settings.

Typical lab studies induce people to either tell the truth or lie. Across several experiments with college students, researchers have accurately classified deceptive communications at a rate of approximately 67 percent (Hancock et al., 2008; Newman et al., 2003; Zhou et al., 2004). Similar rates have been found for classifying truthful and deceptive statements in similar experimental tests among prison inmates (Bond and Lee, 2005). The most consistent language dimensions in identifying truth telling have included use of first-person singular pronouns, exclusive words (e.g., *but, without, except*), higher use of positive emotion words, and lower rates of negative emotion words. Note that the patterns of effects vary somewhat depending on the experimental paradigm.

Correlational real-world studies have found similar patterns. In an unpublished analysis by the second author and Denise Huddle of the courtroom testimony of over 40 people convicted of felonies, those who were later exonerated (approximately half of the sample) showed similar patterns of language markers of truth telling, such as much higher rates of first-person singular pronoun use. A more controversial but interesting real-world example of classifying false and true statements is in the investigation of claims made by Bush administration officials in citing the reasons for the Iraq war. Specifically, Hancock and colleagues (unpublished) examined false statements (e.g., claims that Iraq had weapons of mass destruction or direct links to al-Qaeda) and nonfalse statements (e.g., that Hussein had gassed Iraqis) for words previously found to be associated with deceptive statements. It was found that the statements that had been classified as false contained significantly fewer first-person singular (e.g., *I, me, my*) words and exclusive words (e.g., *but, except, without*) but more negative emotion words (e.g., *angry, hate, terror*) and action verbs (e.g., *lift, push, run*).

Across the various deception studies, the relative rates of word use signaled the underlying psychology of deception. Deception involves less ownership of a story (i.e., fewer first-person singular pronouns) and less complexity (i.e., fewer exclusive words), along with more emotional leakage (i.e., more negative emotion words) and more focus on actions as opposed to intent (i.e., more action verbs). Based on the use of these words, approximately 77 percent of the statements made by the Bush administration were correctly classified as either false or not false. Note that these numbers are likely inflated since estimates of the veracity of statements is dependent on the selection of statements themselves—as opposed to a broader analysis of all statements made by the Bush administration.

It is important to note that the strength of the language model is that it has been applied to a wide variety of natural language samples from low- to high-stakes situations. The degree to which language markers of deception were more pronounced in high-stakes situations relative to low-stakes situations is encouraging. Being able to classify the veracity of high-stakes communications with greater confidence could lead to more efficient allocation of resources for interventions.

Real Threats

A real threat is one that is believed to be true by a speaker or writer, and so linguistic markers of honesty would likely appear in a threatening communication. The next step, then, would be to assess the likelihood of actual behavior. One area in which text analyses have informed psychologists of future behavior is in the written literature and letters of suicidal and nonsuicidal individuals. In one study, Stirman and Pennebaker (2001) analyzed the published works of poets who committed suicide and poets who had not attempted suicide. Poets who committed suicide had used first-person singular pronouns at higher rates in their published poetry than those who did not commit suicide. Poets who committed suicide also used fewer first-person plural pronouns later in their career than did poets who did not commit suicide. Overall, the language used by suicidal poets showed that they were focused more on themselves and were less socially integrated in later life than were nonsuicidal poets. Surprisingly, there were no significant differences in the use of positive and negative emotion words between the two groups and only a marginal effect of greater death-related words used by the poets who committed suicide. Similar effects have been found in later case studies of suicide blogs, letters, and notes (Hui et al., 2009; Stone and Pennebaker, 2004). These results highlight the importance of linguistic style markers (assessed by word count tools) as potentially more psychologically revealing than content words (which would more likely be the focus of judge-based thematic coding).

Stated intentions are not necessarily threats. One area in which follow-through of stated intentions has been studied is in clinical psychology. In psychotherapy, patients typically state an intention to change maladaptive thoughts and behaviors. Mergenthaler (1996) used word counts to identify word categories that characterize key moments in therapy sessions in order to provide an adequate theory of change. He found that key moments of progress are characterized by the co-occurrence of emotion terms and abstractions (i.e., abstract nouns that characterize the intention to reason further about that term) in a case study and in a sample of improved versus nonimproved patients. These suggest that being able to express emotions in a distanced and abstract way is important for therapeutic improvements.

The text analysis programs used by these clinicians, such as Bucci's Discourse Attribute Analysis Program (Bucci and Maskit, 2005), are similar to LIWC in that they use a word count approach and many of their dictionary categories are both grammatical and empirically derived. However, the grammatical categories for the clinical dictionaries are broad (i.e., they throw all function words into a single category), and their empirically derived categories are based on psychoanalytic theories and clinical observations. The advantage of all word count tools for the analysis of therapeutic text is that word counts tend to be a less biased measure of therapeutic improvements than clinician's self-reports (Bucci and Maskit, 2007). In addition, word count tools can be assessed at the turn level, by conversations over time, and for the overall total of all interactions, making word count approaches a powerful tool for assessing follow-through of stated intentions.

Another area in which follow-through of stated intentions has been examined is in weight loss blogs (Chung and Pennebaker, unpublished). Diet blogs were processed using LIWC and assessed for blogging rates and social support. One finding was that cognitive mechanism words (e.g., *understand, realize, should, maybe*) were predictive of quitting the diet blog early and of gaining weight instead of losing weight. This finding was consistent with previous literature which found that attempts at changing self-control behaviors typically fail if an individual is stuck at the precontemplation or contemplation phase of self-change (Prochaska et al., 1992, 1995). Instead, writing in a personal narrative style and actively seeking out social support were predictors of weight loss. Use of cognitive mechanism words, then, can signal flexibility in thinking, and perhaps less resolve, or coming to terms with failure. Since the blogs tracked everyday thoughts and behaviors in a naturalistic environment (i.e., not in a laboratory or clinical study) and were not retrospective reports of the entire self-change process after success or failure, the findings were likely more reflective of the various stages of self-change, instead of a description of a memory of the change. Accounts of a narrative recorded during the time in which an event happened or prospectively instead of simply retrospectively are important in generalizing findings from language studies to threat detection.

Studying the nature of threatening communications can come from the study of terrorist organizations and their communications, as interviews with world terrorists are rare (Post et al., 2009). Note that not all communications by terrorist organizations are threats. However, comparing the natural language of violent and nonviolent groups can tell us about the psychology of groups that will act on their threats (Post et al., 2002). In one study, both computerized word pattern and word count analyses of public statements made by Osama bin Laden and Ayman al-Zawahiri, from the years 1988 through 2006, were examined (Pennebaker and Chung, 2008). Initially, the 58 translated al-Qaeda texts were compared with those of other terrorist groups from a corpus created by Smith (2004). The al-Qaeda texts contained far more hostility as evidenced by their greater use of anger words and third-person plural pronouns.

As for the individual leaders' use of language over time, bin Laden evidenced an increase in his use of positive emotion words as well as negative emotion words, especially anger words. He also showed higher rates of exclusive words (e.g., *but, except, exclude, without*) over the past decade, which often marks cognitive complexity in thinking. On the other hand, al-Zawahiri's statements tended to be slightly more positive, significantly less negative, and less cognitively complex than those of bin Laden. He evidenced a surprising shift in his use of first-person singular pronouns from 2004 to 2006. This was interpreted as indicating greater insecurity, feelings of threat, and perhaps a shift in his relationship with bin Laden. The word count strategy, then, allowed for a close examination of the psychology of the leaders in a way that otherwise would not have been possible.

While much of the above review has been focused on word count approaches, it is worth noting the judge-based thematic analysis approach of Smith et al. (2008) in studying the language of violent and nonviolent groups. Specifically, instead of having a computer count a set of target words, these researchers had trained coders manually interpret and rate the communications of two terrorist groups (central al-Qaeda and al-Qaeda in the Arabian Peninsula) and two comparison groups that did not engage in terrorist violence (Hizb ut-Tahrir and the Movement for Islamic Reform in Arabia). Among some of the complex coding constructs examined were dominance values, which included any statements where subjects were judged to have or want power over others (see Smith, 2003; White, 1951), and affiliation motives, which included statements where subjects were judged to have a concern with establishing, maintaining, or restoring friendly relations with others (see Winter, 1994).

The results from their analyses and the results from previous studies on terrorist and matched control groups (Smith, 2004, 2008) showed some consistent findings. Specifically, the violent groups' communications contained more references to morality, religion/culture, and aggression/dominance. The violent terrorist groups expressed less integrative complexity, more power motive imagery, and more in-group affiliation motive imagery than did the nonviolent groups. These effects were present in the language of violent terrorist groups even before they had engaged in terrorist acts, suggesting that these dimensions could potentially predict the likelihood of violence by a group (Smith, 2004). Further research is needed in order to assess whether these judge-based dimensions will be found at higher rates within a single real threat versus nonthreats from within an organization. In addition, this research would be more suitable for real-time or close to real-time analyses if the judge-based dimensions that are coded at high intercoder reliability rates could reliably be detected using computerized word pattern or word count indices.

Bluffs

Unlike a real threat, a bluff might contain markers of deception since it is one that is believed by the writer or speaker to be false. Although there are many instances of psychologists using deception in laboratory studies to experimentally manipulate states of anxiety, parents threatening to take naughty children to the police, and people threatening to leave their lovers, relatively few studies have examined the word patterns of bluffs.

Although an arguable form of bluffing, several studies have examined the psychology of people who attempt suicide versus those who complete suicide. Some researchers have argued that those who attempt but do not complete suicide have a different motivation—one that is focused on attracting the attention of others (e.g., Farberow and Shneidman, 1961).

If failed attempts at suicide are considered a form of bluffing, it might be thought that the suicide notes of attempters would be different from those of completers. A recent LIWC analysis of notes from 20 attempters and 20 completers found that there were, indeed, significant differences in word use between the two groups. Specifically, completers made more references to positive emotions and social connections and fewer references to death and religion than did attempters. The attempters (or, perhaps, bluffers) appeared to focus more on the suicidal act itself rather than the long-term implications for themselves and others (Handelman and Lester, 2007).

Latent Threats

A latent threat refers to the explicit planning of an aggressive action while at the same time concealing the planned action from the target. In *Godfather* terms this could be an example of keeping one's friends close but one's enemies closer. History, of course, is littered with examples of latent threats—from overtures by Hitler to England and Russia, the Spanish with the Aztecs, and probably most world leaders who have made a decision to go to war. Hogenraad (2003, 2005) and his colleagues (Hogenraad and Garagozav, 2008), for example, used a computer-based motive dictionary (motives that are typically assessed through judge-based thematic coding) to assess the language of leaders during periods of rising conflict. Interestingly, the same pattern of results was found across multiple real-world situations (e.g., in a commented chronology of events leading up to World War II, in Robert F. Kennedy's memoirs of events before the Cuban missile crisis, and in President Saakashvili's speeches during Georgia's recent conflicts with the Russian Federation) and in published fiction (e.g., William Golding's *Lord of the Flies* and Tolstoy's *War and Peace*). It was found that the discrepancy between power and affiliation motives becomes greater as leaders approach wars. Specifically, power motives are identified by words such as *ambition, conservatism, invade, legitimate,* and *recommend*—and increase in times before war. Affiliation motives are identified by such words as *courteous, dad, indifference, mate,* and *thoughtful* and decrease in relation to power motive words before times of war. These results are generally consistent with the findings of Smith et al. (2008) for violent terrorist and nonviolent groups.

An example of a latent threat is that of President George W. Bush's use of first-person singular pronouns during his (over 600) formal and informal press meetings over the course of his presidency (see Figure 1-1). Note that only press interactions in which he was speaking "off the cuff" rather than reading prepared remarks were analyzed. As can be seen in Figure 1-1, there was a large drop in use of the word *I* immediately after

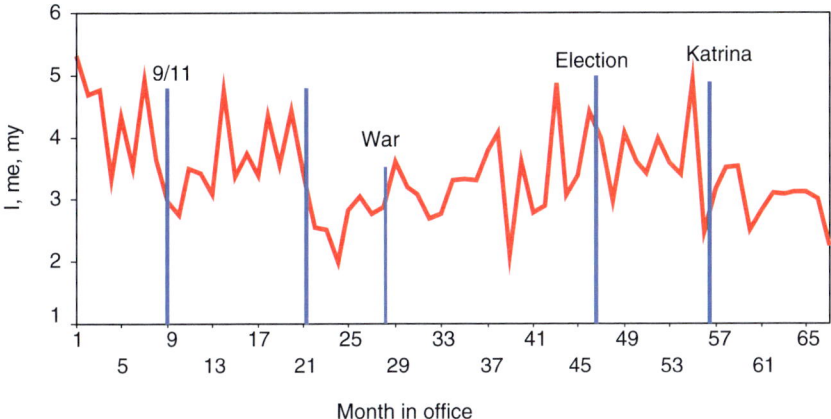

FIGURE 1-1 President George W. Bush's use of first-person singular pronouns during his time in office.

9/11 and again with Hurricane Katrina. Most striking were the drops that began in August 2002, just prior to Senate authorization of the use of force in Iraq. Perhaps this was when President Bush formally decided to go to war in Iraq, an event that caused attention to shift away from himself and on to a task instead. Similarly, the decision to go to war demands a certain degree of secrecy and deception. A leader who does not want to alert the enemy of his intentions must, by definition, talk in a more measured way so as not to reveal hostile intent. Similar observations have been made by other researchers concerning the language that leaders use in planning for wars.[2] If true, one can begin to appreciate how word counts can betray intentions and future actions.

Analysis of the natural language of these political leaders highlights the ability of computerized word counts to reveal how people are attending and responding to their personal upheavals, relationship changes, and world events. A within-subject text analysis of public speeches over time bypassed the difficulties in traditional self-reports (i.e., personally seeking out these leaders in their top-secret hideouts to ask them to fill out questionnaires with minimal response biases).

---

[2]R. Hogenraad, Catholic University of Louvain, Belgium, personal communication [June 2003].

Nonthreats and the Nature of Genres

As noted earlier, text analysis of nonthreats is conceptually similar to study of a control group. In other words, most studies on threats have relied on a nonthreat control group. Such a group assumes a reasonable degree of honesty in the communication stream. Ironically, any discussion of a nonthreat group raises a series of additional questions about the defining feature of honest communications.

People use language differently depending on the context of their speech. A person talking with a close friend uses language differently than when making an address to a nation. Communicating to a hostile audience typically involves a different set of words and sentence constructions than when speaking to admirers. Any computer analysis of threatening communication must take into account the context. For example, there is reason to believe that, for some people, honest formal speech can look remarkably similar to dishonest more informal language.

A comparison of word use as a function of genres was first reported in a pioneering study by Biber (1988). Using a factor analytic approach to word use, he found that different forms of writing (e.g., news stories, romance novels, telephone conversations) each had their own unique linguistic fingerprint. The present authors have amassed hundreds of thousands of texts spanning dozens of genres and found striking differences that reflect genre, the demographics of the speaker (e.g., age, sex, social class), the relationship between speaker and listener, and so forth (see Pennebaker et al., 2003; Chung and Pennebaker, 2007).

FUTURE DIRECTIONS

The use of text analysis to understand the psychology of threatening communications is just beginning. A small but growing number of experts in social/cognitive/personality psychology, communications, linguistics, computational linguistics, and computer science have only recently begun to realize the importance of linking relatively low level language use to much broader culture-relevant phenomena. Indeed, there is a sense that we are on the threshold of a paradigm shift in the social sciences. As can be gleaned from this review, very little research, to date, has focused specifically on computerized text analysis of threats. Several challenges and suggestions for future research are outlined below.

Practical and Structural Hurdles

For language research to reach the next level, a number of practical questions must be addressed. Many of these call for greater cooperation

Cross-Discipline Cooperation

Cross-disciplinary and cross-institution research can lead to an exponential growth in understanding and predicting threatening behaviors. The ability to address socially relevant questions using large data banks will require the close cooperation of psychologists, computer scientists, and computational linguists in academia and in private companies. The ability to find, retrieve, store, and analyze large and quickly changing datasets requires expertise across multiple domains.

Creation of Shared-Text Databases

A pressing practical issue that must be addressed is access to data. First, by increasing access to data from naturally occurring threats from forensic investigations and across laboratories, researchers can start to build a more complete picture of threatening communications and compare text analytic methods in terms of their efficacy for assessing threat features. A consortium or text bank would have to include transcribed threats of all genres, across various modalities, of varying stakes, and in multiple languages, along with annotations for common features with other corpora in the text bank. In addition, the text bank would need to include language samples from nonthreats, such as transcripts for spoken language in everyday life (e.g., Mehl et al., 2001). The text bank could potentially be updated with annotations from study results, such as classification rates, psychological characteristics, and new findings as they are produced.

The collection and maintenance of a large threat-related data bank must include data from four very different types of sources. The first is an *Internet base* made up of hundreds of thousands of blogs and other frequently changing text samples. As potential threats appear in different parts of the world, a database that reflects the thoughts and feelings of a large group of people can be invaluable in learning the degree to which any socially shared upheaval is reflecting and/or leading a societal shift in attention or attitudes. Comparable publicly available databases should also be built for newspapers, letters to the editor, and so forth. These databases should be updated in near real time.

A second database should be a *threat communications base*. Some of the contents might be classified, but most should be open source. Such a database would include speeches, letters, historical communications, and position statements of leaders and formal and informal institutions. The database should include a corpus of individual-level threats—ransom notes, telephone transcripts, television interview transcripts—that can provide insight into how people threaten others. Such a database should also provide transcripts and background information on the people or groups being threatened.

A third database should include *natural language samples*. To date, very few real-world samples of people talking actually exist. The closest are transcribed telephone calls (as part of the Linguistic Data Consortium; see, e.g., Liberman, 2009), which are recorded in controlled laboratory settings. One strategy that has promise concerns use of the Electronic Activated Recorder (EAR; see, e.g., Mehl et al., 2001)—a digital recorder that can record for 30 seconds every 12 to 13 minutes for several days. Mehl and others have now amassed daily recordings of hundreds of people, all of which have been transcribed. Using technologies such as the EAR, we can ultimately get natural instances of a broad range of human interactions, including those that involve threats.

Finally, threat-related *experimental laboratory studies* must be run and archived. A significant concern of the large-database approach to linking language with threatening communications is that it is ultimately correlational. That is, we can see how events can influence language changes. Similarly, we can determine how the language of one person may ultimately predict behaviors. The problem is that this approach is generally unable to determine if language is a causal variable. A president, for example, might use the pronoun *I* less often before going to war. However, the drop in *I* is not the reason or causal agent for the war. Curious social scientists will want to know what the drops signify. Such questions are most efficiently answered with laboratory experiments. An experimental laboratory study database could include both language samples from studies and any other data collected from the studies for further annotations.

Beyond the Words: Personality, Social Relationships, and Mental Health

On the surface, it might seem that the study of threatening communications should focus most heavily on the communications themselves. Indeed, it is important to know about the components of written or spoken threats. However, threats are made by individuals to other individuals within particular social contexts. It is critical that any language analyses of threatening communications explore the individual differences of the threateners and the threatened within the social context of the interactions.

To better assess the relationships between personality and language, individuals of all ages, socioeconomic status, and cultures must be sampled, along with any language samples that can be acquired from political leaders (e.g., Hart, 1984; Post, 2005; Suedfeld, 1994; Slatcher et al., 2007). Researchers should be encouraged to track threats that occur in everyday life. It is known from over 20 years of research studies conducted worldwide that, when asked to write about their deepest thoughts and feelings about a traumatic event, participants are often very willing to disclose vivid and personal details about highly stigmatizing traumas, such as disfigurement, the death of a loved one, incest, and rape (for a review, see Pennebaker and Chung, 2007). The ability to collect naturalistic evidence of long-term secrets and deception, then, is promising. Studies might come, for example, from e-mail records from individuals in the community who had kept a secret from a spouse, a lover, friends, or their boss that implied various levels of harm. Academics might also explore threats across various modalities in order to tap how a particular community or population experiences widespread threats, for example, from blogs, newspaper articles, or telephone calls (see Cohn et al., 2001, and Pennebaker and Chung, 2005).

There has been much research showing that the odds of violent or approach behavior increase when mental illness is present (Dietz et al., 1991; Douglas et al., 2009; Fazel et al., 2009; James et al., 2007, 2008, 2009; Mullen et al., 2008; Warren et al., 2007). Once empirical research has reliably identified the linguistic features of mental illness, future research can investigate the degree to which threats are communicated by individuals with various mental illnesses and disorders.

Culture and Language

Threats can come from individuals and groups of varying languages and cultures. The ability to assess a threatening communication in the same language it was produced is important because there are no perfect translations. Such communications must also be assessed within the context of cultural experts. Below, a text analytic approach is described that the present authors are developing to assess the psychology of speakers from other cultures and determine which features are lost or gained in translations.

The use of LIWC in psychological studies has extended beyond the United States, where it was originally developed. This has been made possible because the software includes a feature for the user to select an external dictionary to reference when analyzing text files. This feature, along with the ability of LIWC2007 to process Unicode text, has enabled processing of texts in many other languages. Currently, there are validated dictionaries available in Spanish (Ramirez-Esparza et al., 2007), German

(Wolf et al., 2008), Dutch, Norwegian, Italian, and Korean. Versions in Chinese, French, Hungarian, Russian, and Turkish are in various phases of development. Note that each of these dictionaries has been developed using the LIWC2001 (Pennebaker et al., 2001) or LIWC2007 default dictionary categorization scheme. That is, words in other languages have been forced into the English language categorization scheme used in the LIWC2001 or LIWC2007 default dictionaries.

During the Arabic translation of the English default dictionary, the present authors and their colleagues also began to develop the first LIWC dictionary that was categorized entirely according to a foreign language's grammatical scheme. Specifically, we created a LIWC dictionary according to an Arabic grammatical scheme (Hayeri et al., unpublished). Next, the dictionary was translated into English to make an English version of LIWC that would impose an Arabic categorization scheme onto English texts. Because each language affords somewhat different types of information, we should be able to see how the two languages provide different insights into the same texts. These sets of dictionaries have many potential applications in cross-cultural psychology, computational linguistics, and forensic psychology.

In the case of cross-cultural psychology, demographic or psychological characteristics could be assessed in translations or in documents for which the original language is unknown. With further validation work for language style markers for psychological features such as deception or psychopathy across translations, researchers who are familiar with only the English language could conduct analyses of foreign language texts using translations into English. News articles from a given Middle Eastern region could be assessed for demographic or psychological characteristics, without full proficiency in the original language of the article. Of course, having cultural experts on hand to understand the greater social context of any communication in which it originally occurred is important, but text analyses can sometimes offer an unbiased look at a given text.

In the case of computational linguistics, finding out whether, for example, language markers of sex differences are maintained in translations between Arabic and English could aid in investigations of author identification for translated documents. Note that computerized word patterning methods have already been successfully applied to authorship identification and characterization for Arabic and English extremist-group Web forums (Abbasi and Chen, 2005).

In the case of forensic psychology, if a translated text is presented to a researcher, it might be difficult to assess the demographic or psychological characteristics of the author if the author's original text or language skills are unavailable or inaccessible. In another example, consider the case where some documents are available for a given subject in Arabic, while other documents are available only as English language translations. By using the set of Arabic LIWC dictionaries, it would be possible to assess certain features of language style in both texts and treat them as equivalent or be cautious in doing so in order to maximize the use of all available documents without translations. In forensic investigations this may be the case: Captured or overheard communications may be available in a given language, but more public communications might be more readily available in English. Having the set of dictionaries to combine the language samples could maximize the degree to which the results are reliable and representative of communications from a particular individual or group.

Clearly, more validation work is required to assess the use of the Arabic LIWC dictionaries for cross-language investigations. However, the approach laid out here can help in beginning to see the world through Arabic and English eyes using a simple word counting program for assessing language style. Although it is currently rare, some multidisciplinary labs have come together using a rapprochement of text analytic techniques to provide a more complete psychological profile in cross-language investigations (Graesser et al., 2009; Hancock et al., 2010). Future multidisciplinary research in cross-language investigations is encouraged.

Automated Classifiers: Social Language Processing

The language features reported here have been shown to be predictors for a variety of behaviors. However, in assessing the value of the findings and determining how they can be applied in future investigations of actual cases of predicting behaviors, a larger framework for systematically applying language techniques to behaviors is needed. The following section describes an interdisciplinary paradigm that seeks to build an automated classifier for predicting behaviors from natural language. Specifically, Hancock et al.'s 2010 Social Language Processing (SLP) paradigm, which represents a rapprochement of tools, techniques, and theories from computational linguistics, communications, discourse processing, and social and personality psychology, is described.

SLP has only recently been introduced by Hancock et al. (2010) as a paradigm for predicting behaviors from language. Broadly, it consists of three stages: (1) linguistic feature identification, (2) linguistic feature extraction, and (3) statistical classifier development. The first stage, linguistic feature identification, involves finding theoretical or empirically known grammatical or psychological features of language at the word or phrase level that might be associated with the behavior or construct in question. Hancock et al. (2010) gave the example of first-person singular pronouns, or *I*, in the case of deception, since liars tend to divert focus from themselves in a lie. In the second stage, linguistic feature extraction, texts whose social features are known are examined for the language feature from stage 1. In the case of deception, court transcripts (described earlier), laboratory studies (e.g., Newman et al., 2003), and political speeches (e.g., Hancock et al., unpublished) known to include deceptive and nondeceptive texts have been assessed for rates of first-person singular pronoun use, it has been shown that lies are indeed associated with a decrease in *I* usage (for a review, see Hancock et al., 2008).

Finally, in the third stage, classifier development, a series of stages is used to classify texts according to the social construct in question and to automatically and inductively assess texts for additional language features that might improve classifier performance. Again, returning to the case of deception, the classifiers would be run on documents known to be deceptive or not, additional features that predict deception could be assessed, and then future documents of unknown verity could be assessed using the same classifier for the probability that the new document is deceptive or not.

Note that there are several features of SLP that make it a suitable approach to be developed and applied for investigations of threatening communications and actual behavior. First, SLP is empirically based. That is, SLP draws from theories and case studies and from previous and continuing research on large numbers of texts.

Second, SLP learns. Each of SLP's stages can inform the others and be recursive, meaning that the classifier for each construct can be continually improved for accuracy and detection of features with additional data. For example, in the third stage, classifier development, the unsupervised machine learning techniques for inductively identifying linguistic features associated with a given construct can be especially helpful in examining communications in another language for which linguistic features signaling a social or psychological construct are as yet unknown (Hancock et al., 2010).

Third, SLP is probabilistic. In the prediction of behaviors, only probabilistic, not absolute, predictions can be made. To say that there are only a few features that predict a particular behavior and that these are completely and accurately conveyed through a set of known language features would oversimplify the complexities of human behavior and the ways in which natural language is produced. In the case of deception, human judges can barely assess deception above chance levels regardless of expertise or confidence in making such assessments (Newman et al., 2003; Vrij, 2008). Word counts have detected deception at rates that are much higher than chance (approximately 67 to 77 percent). Even these rates should not be taken too seriously. Most laboratory-based deception studies are conducted in a gamelike atmosphere, where the experimenters maintain tight control over the information and setting and rely on participants who are typically quite similar to one another and where a ground truth of 50 percent is known. The regularities found in deceptive communications even within highly curated datasets are probabilistic and with considerable error, requiring even greater caution when identifying deception in the real world. Any models of predicting behaviors must be evaluated by the rates at which they can accurately classify behaviors above chance occurrence (i.e., 50 percent) in more complicated real-world settings.

Finally, SLP is deliverable. That is, the tools and techniques that SLP uses to identify and to assess linguistic features for a given construct are the same tools and techniques that would be applied to a new document. These tools and techniques are mostly free and publicly available or can be purchased online for a couple hundred dollars. The techniques require some programming skills, but these steps can be made into a Windows-based program by which most any layperson could upload a document and the computer would display a number associated with the probability that the document is either x or y (e.g., likely to lead to actual behavior or not). This is especially important for real-time or close to real-time investigations of threatening communications for which interventions are needed immediately. Note, again, that the ultimate contribution of text analyses of threatening communications will come from the degree to which text analysis informs us about the underlying psychology of the actors.

CONCLUSION

There has been little work so far on computerized text analysis of threatening communications. Nevertheless, several studies across several disciplines have demonstrated that word use is reliably linked to psychological states and that the underlying psychology of a speaker or author can be revealed through text analysis. With continued research on the basic relationships between natural language use and psychological states, a shared open-source or consortium-style text bank on threatening communications and a multidisciplinary effort in building models to assess the probability of harm arising from threats, much progress can be made. In assessing a threatening communication it is important to understand the psychology of the threat's deliverer and receiver, especially in light of the culture in which it occurs. Our responses to threats, then, can be better informed, as threatening communications dynamically unfold. With the use of text analytic tools, quick and reliable assessments and interventions may be possible.

REFERENCES

Abbasi, A., and H. Chen. 2005. Applying authorship analysis to extremist-group Web forum messages. *IEEE Intelligent Systems*, 20(5):67-75.

Adams, S.H. 2002. Communication Under Stress: Indicators of Veracity and Deception in Written Narratives. Unpublished doctoral dissertation, Virginia Polytechnic Institute and State University, Blacksburg.

Adams, S. 2004. Statement analysis: Beyond the words. *FBI Law Enforcement Bulletin*, 73(April):22-23.

Atkinson, J.W., and D.C. McClelland. 1948. The projective expression of needs. II. The effect of different intensities of hunger drive on Thematic Apperception. *Journal of Experimental Psychology*, 38(6):643-658.

Biber, D. 1988. *Variation Across Speech and Writing*. Cambridge, UK: Cambridge University Press.

Biber, D., S. Conrad, and R. Reppen. 1998. *Corpus Linguistics: Investigating Language Structure and Use*. Cambridge, UK: Cambridge University Press.

Bond, G.D., and A.Y. Lee. 2005. Language of lies in prison: Linguistic classification of prisoners' truthful and deceptive natural language. *Applied Cognitive Psychology*, 19(3):313-329.

Bucci, W., and B. Maskit. 2005. Building a weighted dictionary for referential activity. In Y. Qu, J.G. Shanahan, and J. Wiebe, eds., *Computing Attitude and Affect in Text* (pp. 49-60). Dordrecht, The Netherlands: Springer.

Bucci, W., and B. Maskit. 2007. Beneath the surface of the therapeutic interaction: The psychoanalytic method in modern dress. *Journal of the American Psychoanalytic Association*, 55:1355-1397.

Burgoon, J.K., and D.B. Buller. 2008. Interpersonal deception theory. In L. A. Baxter and D. O. Braithewaite, eds., *Engaging Theories in Interpersonal Communication: Multiple Perspectives* (pp. 227-239). Thousand Oaks, CA: Sage Publications.

Buss, D.M., ed. 2005. *The Handbook of Evolutionary Psychology*. Hoboken, NJ: John Wiley and Sons.

Chung, C.K., and J.W. Pennebaker. 2007. The psychological functions of function words. In K. Fiedler, ed., *Social Communication* (pp. 343-359). New York: Psychology Press.

Chung, C.K., and J.W. Pennebaker. 2008. Revealing dimensions of thinking in open-ended self-descriptions: An automated meaning extraction method for natural language. *Journal of Research in Personality*, 42:96-132.

Chung, C.K., and J.W. Pennebaker. Unpublished. Predicting weight loss in blogs using computerized text analysis. Derived from Ph.D. thesis of the same name, by C.K. Chung. Available: http://repositories.lib.utexas.edu/bitstream/handle/2152/6541/chungc16811.pdf?sequence=2 [accessed October 2010].

Chung, C.K., C. Jones, A. Liu, and J.W. Pennebaker. 2008. Predicting success and failure in weight loss blogs through natural language use. *Proceedings of the International Conference on Weblogs and Social Media (ICWSM 2008)*, pp. 180-181.

Cohn, M.A., M.R. Mehl, and J.W. Pennebaker. 2001. Linguistic markers of psychological change surrounding September 11, 2001. *Psychological Science*, 15:687-693.

Dietz, P.E., D.B. Matthews, C. Van Duyne, D.A. Martell, C.D.H. Parry, T. Stewart, J. Warren, and J.D. Crowder. 1991. Threatening and otherwise inappropriate letters to Hollywood celebrities. *Journal of Forensic Sciences*, 36:185-209.

Douglas, K.S., L.S. Guy, and S.D. Hart. 2009. Psychosis as a risk factor for violence to others: A meta-analysis. *Psychological Bulletin*, 135(5):679-706.

Farberow, N.L., and E.S. Shneidman, eds. 1961. *The Cry for Help*. New York: McGraw-Hill.

Fazel, S., G. Gulati, L. Linsell, J.R. Geddes, and M. Grann. 2009. Schizophrenia and violence: Systematic review and meta-analysis. *PLoS Med*, 6(8):1-15, article number e1000120.

Fazio, R.H., and M.A. Olson. 2003. Implicit measures in social cognition research: Their meaning and use. *Annual Review of Psychology,* 54:297-327.

Foltz, P.W. 1996. Latent semantic analysis for text-based research. *Behavior Research Methods, Instruments and Computers,* 28(2):197-202.

Gottschalk, L.A. 1997. The unobtrusive measurement of psychological states and traits. In C.W. Roberts, ed., *Text Analysis for the Social Sciences: Methods for Drawing Statistical Inferences from Texts and Transcripts* (pp. 117-129). Mahwah, NJ: Erlbaum.

Gottschalk, L.A., M.K. Stein, and D.H. Shapiro. 1997. The application of computerized content analysis of speech to the diagnostic process in a psychiatric outpatient clinic. *Journal of Clinical Psychology,* 53(5):427-441.

Graesser, A.C., D.S. McNamara, M.M. Louwerse, and Z. Cai. 2004. Coh-Metrix: Analysis of text on cohesion and language. *Behavioral Research Methods, Instruments, and Computers,* 36:193-202.

Graesser, A.C., L. Han, M. Jeon, J. Myers, J. Kaltner, Z. Cai, P. McCarthy, L. Shala, M. Louwerse, X. Hu, V. Rus, D. McNamara, J. Hancock, C. Chung, and J. Pennebaker. 2009. Cohesion and classification of speech acts in Arabic discourse. Paper presented at the Society for Text and Discourse, Rotterdam, The Netherlands.

Hall, J.A., E.J. Coats, and L. Smith LeBeau. 2005. Nonverbal behavior and the vertical dimension of social relations: A meta-analysis. *Psychological Bulletin,* 131(6):898-924.

Hancock, J.T., L. Curry, S. Goorha, and M.T. Woodworth. 2008. On lying and being lied to: A linguistic analysis of deception. *Discourse Processes,* 45(1):1-23.

Hancock, J.T., D.I. Beaver, C.K. Chung, J. Frazee, J.W. Pennebaker, A.C. Graesser, and Z. Cai. 2010. Social language processing: A framework for analyzing the communication of terrorists and authoritarian regimes. *Behavioral Sciences in Terrorism and Political Aggression, Special Issue: Memory and Terrorism,* 2:108-132.

Hancock, J.T., N.N. Bazarova, and D. Markowitz. Unpublished. A linguistic analysis of Bush administration statements on Iraq. J.T. Hancock, Department of Communication, Cornell University.

Handelman, L.D., and D. Lester. 2007. The content of suicide notes from attempters and completers. *Crisis,* 28(2):102-104.

Hart, R.P. 1984. *Verbal Style and the Presidency: A Computer-Based Analysis.* New York: Academic Press.

Hayeri, N., C.K. Chung, and J.W. Pennebaker. Unpublished. Computer-based text analysis across cultures: Viewing language samples through English and Arabic eyes. C.K. Chung and J.W. Pennebaker, Department of Psychology, University of Texas, Austin.

Heckhausen, H. 1963. Eine Rahmentheorie der Motivation in zehn Thesen [A theoretical framework of motivation in 10 theses]. *Zeitschrift für Experimentelle und Angewandte Psychologie,* 10:604-626.

Hogenraad, R. 2003. The words that predict the outbreak of wars. *Empirical Studies of the Arts,* 21:5-20.

Hogenraad, R. 2005. What the words of war can tell us about the risk of war. *Peace and Conflict: Journal of Peace Psychology,* 11(2):137-151.

Hogenraad, R., and R. Garagozov. 2008. *The Age of Divergence: Georgia and the Lost Certainties of the West.* Report to the Sixth General Meeting, World Public Forum, "Dialogue of Civilizations," Rhodes, Greece.

Hui, N.H.H., V.W.K. Tang, G.H.H. Wu, and B.C.P. Lam. 2009. ON-line to OFF-life? Linguistic comparison of suicide completer and attempter's online diaries. Paper presented at the International Conference on Psychology in Modern Cities, Hong Kong.

James, D.V., P.E. Mullen, J.R. Meloy, M.T. Pathe, F.R. Farnham, L. Preston, and B. Darnley. 2007. The role of mental disorder in attacks on European politicians, 1990-2004. *Acta Psychiatry Scandinavia,* 116:334-344.

James, D.V., P.E. Mullen, M.T. Pathe, J.R. Meloy, F.R. Farnham, L. Preston, and B. Darnley. 2008. Attacks on the British Royal Family: The role of psychotic illness. *Journal of the American Academy of Psychiatry and Law*, 36(1):59-67.

James, D.V., P.E. Mullen, M.T. Pathe, J.R. Meloy, L.F. Preston, B. Darnley, and F.R. Farnham. 2009. Stalkers and harassers of royalty: The role of mental illness and motivation. *Psychological Medicine*, 39(9):1479-1490.

Junghaenel, D.U., J.M. Smyth, and L. Santner. 2008. Linguistic dimensions of psychopathology: A quantitative analysis. *Journal of Social and Clinical Psychology*, 27(1):36-55.

Landauer, T.K., and S.T. Dumais. 1997. A solution to Plato's problem: The latent semantic analysis theory of acquisition, induction, and representation of knowledge. *Psychological Review*, 104(2):211-240.

Landauer, T.K., P.W. Foltz, and D. Laham. 1998. An introduction to latent semantic analysis. *Discourse Processes*, 25(2-3):259-284.

Liberman, M. 2009. *The Linguistic Data Consortium*. Philadelphia: University of Pennsylvania. Available: http://www.ldc.upenn.edu [accessed April 2010].

McAdams, D.P. 2001. The psychology of life stories. *Review of General Psychology*, 5(2):100-122.

Mehl, M., J.W. Pennebaker, D.M. Crow, J. Dabbs, and J. Price. 2001. The Electronically Activated Recorder (EAR): A device for sampling naturalistic daily activities and conversations. *Behavior Research Methods, Instruments, and Computers*, 33(4):517-523.

Mehl, M.R., S.D. Gosling, and J.W. Pennebaker. 2006. Personality in its natural habitat: Manifestations and implicit folk theories of personality in daily life. *Journal of Personality and Social Psychology*, 90:862-877.

Mergenthaler, E. 1996. Emotion-abstraction patterns in verbatim protocols: A new way of describing psychotherapeutic processes. *Journal of Consulting and Clinical Psychology*, 64(6):1306-1315.

Mullen, P.E., D.V. James, J.R. Meloy, M.T. Pathe, F.R. Farnham, L. Preston, and B. Darnley. 2008. The role of psychotic illness in attacks on public figures. In J.R. Meloy, L. Sheridan, and J. Hoffman, eds., *Stalking, Threatening and Attacking Public Figures* (pp. 55-82). New York, NY: Oxford University Press.

Newman, M.L., J.W. Pennebaker, D.S. Berry, and J.M. Richards. 2003. Lying words: Predicting deception from linguistic style. *Personality and Social Psychology Bulletin*, 29(5):665-675.

Newman, M.L., C.J. Groom, L.D. Handelman, and J.W. Pennebaker. 2008. Gender differences in language use: An analysis of 14,000 text samples. *Discourse Processes*, 45:211-246.

Oberlander, J., and A.J. Gill. 2006. Language with character: A stratified corpus comparison of individual differences in e-mail communication. *Discourse Processes*, 42(3):239-270.

Oxman, T.E., S.D. Rosenberg, P.P. Schnurr, and G.J. Tucker. 1982. Diagnostic classification through content analysis of patients' speech. *American Journal of Psychiatry*, 145:464-468.

Pennebaker, J.W., and C.K. Chung. 2005. Tracking the social dynamics of responses to terrorism: Language, behavior, and the Internet. In S. Wessely and V.N. Krasnov, eds., *Psychological Responses to the New Terrorism: A NATO Russia Dialogue* (pp. 159-170). Amsterdam, The Netherlands: IOS Press.

Pennebaker, J.W., and C.K. Chung. 2007. Expressive writing, emotional upheavals, and health. In H. Friedman and R. Silver, eds., *Handbook of Health Psychology* (pp. 263-284). New York: Oxford University Press.

Pennebaker, J.W., and C.K. Chung. 2008. Computerized text analysis of al-Qaeda statements. In K. Krippendorff and M. Bock, eds., *A Content Analysis Reader* (pp. 453-466). Thousand Oaks, CA: Sage.

Pennebaker, J.W., and L.A. King. 1999. Linguistic styles: Language use as an individual difference. *Journal of Personality and Social Psychology*, 77(6):1296-1312.

Pennebaker, J.W., and L.D. Stone. 2003. Words of wisdom: Language use over the lifespan. *Journal of Personality and Social Psychology*, 85:291-301.

Pennebaker, J.W., M.E. Francis, and R.J. Booth. 2001. *Linguistic Inquiry and Word Count: LIWC 2001*. Mahwah, NJ: Erlbaum Publishers.

Pennebaker, J.W., M.R. Mehl, and K. Niederhoffer. 2003. Psychological aspects of natural language use: Our words, our selves. *Annual Review of Psychology,* 54:547-577.

Pennebaker, J.W., R.J. Booth, and M.E. Francis. 2007. *Linguistic Inquiry and Word Count (LIWC2007)*. Available: http://www.liwc.net [accessed April 2010].

Peterson, C. 1992. Explanatory style: Motivation and personality. In C.P. Smith, J.W. Atkinson, D.C. McClelland, and J. Veroff, eds., *Handbook of Thematic Content Analysis* (pp. 376-382). New York: Cambridge University Press.

Poppin, R. 2000. *Computer-Assisted Text Analysis*. Thousand Oaks, CA: Sage Publications.

Post, J.M. 2005. *The Psychological Assessment of Political Leaders: With Profiles of Saddam Hussein and Bill Clinton*. Ann Arbor, MI: University of Michigan Press.

Post, J.M., K.G. Ruby, and E.D. Shaw. 2002. The radical group in context: 1. An integrated framework for the analysis of group risk for terrorism. *Studies in Conflict and Terrorism,* 25(2):73-100.

Post, J.M., E. Sprinzak, and L.M. Denny. 2009. The terrorists in their own words: Interviews with incarcerated Middle Eastern terrorists. In J. Victoroff and A.W. Kruglanski, eds., *Psychology of Terrorism: Classic and Contemporary Insights* (pp. 109-117). New York: Psychology Press.

Prochaska, J.O., C.C. DiClemente, and J.C. Norcross. 1992. In search of how people change: Applications to addictive behaviors. *American Psychologist,* 47(9):1102-1114.

Prochaska, J.O., J.C. Norcross, and C.C. DiClemente. 1995. *Changing for Good*. New York: Avon.

Ramirez-Esparza, N., J.W. Pennebaker, A.F. Garcia, and R. Suria. 2007. La psicologia del uso de las palabras: Un programa de computadora que analiza textos en Espanol [The psychology of word use: A computer program that analyzes text in Spanish]. *Revista Mexicana de Psicologia,* 24:85-99.

Ramirez-Esparza, N., C.K. Chung, E. Kacewicz, and J.W. Pennebaker. 2008. The psychology of word use in depression forums in English and in Spanish: Testing two text analytic approaches. *Proceedings of the 2008 International Conference on Weblogs and Social Media,* pp. 102-108, Menlo Park, CA: The AAAI Press.

Ramirez-Esparza, N., C.K. Chung, G. Sierra-Otero, and J.W. Pennebaker. (in press). Cross-constructions of self: American and Mexican college students. *Journal of Cross-Cultural Psychology*.

Semin, G.R., M. Rubini, and K. Fiedler. 1995. The answer is in the question: The effect of verb causality upon locus of explanation. *Personality and Social Psychology Bulletin,* 21:834-842.

Slatcher, R.B., C.K. Chung, J.W. Pennebaker, and L.D. Stone. 2007. Winning words: Individual differences in linguistic style among U.S. presidential candidates. *Journal of Research in Personality,* 41:63-75.

Smith, A.G. 2003. From words to action: Exploring the relationship between a group's value references and its tendency to engage in terrorism. Unpublished doctoral dissertation, University of Michigan, Ann Arbor.

Smith, A.G. 2004. From words to action: Exploring the relationship between a group's value references and its likelihood of engaging in terrorism. *Studies in Conflict and Terrorism,* 27:409-437.

Smith, A.G. 2008. The implicit motives of terrorist groups: How the needs for affiliation and power translate into death and destruction. *Political Psychology,* 29(1):55-75.

Smith, A.G., P. Sudefeld, L.G. Conway III, and D.G. Winter. 2008. The language of violence: Distinguishing terrorist from nonterrorist groups by thematic content analysis. *Dynamics of Assymetric Conflict,* 1(2):142-163.

Stein, N.L., and E.R. Albro. 1997. Building complexity and coherence: Children's use of goal-structured knowledge in telling stories. In M.G. Bamberg, ed., *Narrative Development: Six Approaches* (pp. 5-44). Mahwah, NJ: Lawrence Erlbaum Associates.

Steyvers, M., and T. Griffiths. 2007. Probabilistic topic models. In T. Landauer, D. McNamara, S. Dennis, and W. Kintsch, eds., *Latent Semantic Analysis: A Road to Meaning* (pp. 427-448). Mahwah, NJ: Lawrence Erlbaum Associates.

Stirman, S.W., and J.W. Pennebaker. 2001. Word use in the poetry of suicidal and non-suicidal poets. *Psychosomatic Medicine*, 63:517-522.

Stone, L.D., and J.W. Pennebaker. 2004. What was she trying to say? A linguistic analysis of Katie's diaries. In D. Lester, ed., *Katie's Diary: Unlocking the Mystery of a Suicide* (pp. 55-80). London, UK: Taylor and Francis.

Suedfeld, P. 1994. President Clinton's policy dilemmas: A cognitive analysis. *Political Psychology*, 15:337-349.

Suedfeld, P., P.E. Tetlock, and S. Streufert. 1992. Conceptual/integrative complexity. In C.P. Smith, J.W. Atkinson, D.C. McClelland, and J. Veroff, eds., *Handbook of Thematic Content Analysis* (pp. 393-400). New York: Cambridge University Press.

Tannen, D. 1993. *Framing in Discourse*. London, UK: Oxford University Press.

Tausczik, Y.R., and J.W. Pennebaker. 2010. The psychological meaning of words: LIWC and computerized text analysis methods. *Journal of Language and Social Psychology*, 29(1): 24-54.

Tsai, J.L., D.I. Simeonova, and J.T. Watanabe. 2004. Somatic and social: Chinese Americans talk about emotion. *Personality and Social Psychology Bulletin*, 30(9):1226-1238.

Vrij, A. 2000. *Detecting Lies and Deceit: The Psychology of Lying and Its Implications for Professional Practice*. Chichester, UK: John Wiley and Sons.

Vrij, A. 2008. *Detecting Lies and Deceit: Pitfalls and Opportunities*. Chichester, UK: John Wiley and Sons.

Warren, L.J., P.E. Mullen, S.D.M. Thomas, J.R.P. Ogloff, and P.M. Burgess. 2007. Threats to kill: A follow-up study. *Psychological Medicine*, 38(4):599-605.

White, R.K. 1951. *Value-Analysis: Nature and Use of the Method*. Ann Arbor, MI: Society of the Psychological Study of Social Issues.

Winter, D.G. 1991. Measuring personality at a distance: Development of an integrated system for scoring motives in running text. In A.J. Stewart, J.M. Healy, Jr., and D.J. Ozer, eds., *Perspectives in Personality: Approaches to Understanding Lives* (pp. 59-89). London, UK: Jessica Kingsley Publishers.

Winter, D.G. 1994. *Manual for Scoring Motive Imagery in Running Text*. Ann Arbor, MI: Department of Psychology, University of Michigan.

Wolf, M., A.B. Horn, M.R. Mehl, S. Haug, J.W. Pennebaker, and H. Kordy. 2008. Computer-gestuetzte quantitative Textanalyse: Aequivalenz und Robustheit der deutschen Version des Linguistic Inquiry and Word Count [Computerized quantitative text analysis: Equivalence and robustness of the German adaptation of Linguistic Inquiry and Word Count]. *Diagnostica*, 54:85-98.

Wolf, M., C.K. Chung, and H. Kordy. 2010a. Inpatient treatment to online aftercare: E-mailing themes as a function of therapeutic outcomes. *Psychotherapy Research*, 20(1):71-85.

Wolf, M., C.K. Chung, and H. Kordy. 2010b. MEM's search for meaning: A rejoinder. *Psychotherapy Research*, 20(1):93-99.

Zhou, L., J.K. Burgoon, D. Twitchell, T. Qin, and J.F. Nunamaker. 2004. A comparison of classification methods for predicting deception in computer-mediated communication. *Journal of Management Information Systems*, 20(4):139-165.

Communication-Based Research Related to Threats and Ensuing Behavior

H. Dan O'Hair, Daniel Rex Bernard, and Randy R. Roper

"Those that are the loudest in their threats are the weakest in their actions."

Charles Caleb Colton (1780–1832)
British clergyman, sportsman, and author

INTRODUCTION

A threatening communication is any message that "implies or explicitly states the potential of harm delivered to targets/victims or agents acting on their behalf" (Smith, 2008b, p. 106). Understandably, risk assessment efforts analyze and evaluate direct threats and the potential for violent behavior they represent. However, research indicates that threat assessment endeavors should not be limited only to communications that contain explicit threats.

Frequently, those who pose legitimate threats do not actually communicate their intentions. According to Fein and Vossekuil (1998), few assassins or attackers send direct threats to their intended targets or to law enforcement, but as many as two-thirds are known to speak or write about their intentions to others. Such violent intentions are disclosed to family, friends, or co-workers or are written about in personal journals. Recent technological trends suggest that such alarming communicative behaviors may also appear online via Internet blogs, message boards, and virtual chat rooms (e.g., Willard, 2007). Therefore, since indirect communications expressing violent intentions often exist, threat assessment efforts should target indirect as well as explicit threatening messages by would-be attackers.

A more inclusive approach would consider multiple communicative activities by the potential perpetrator(s), consistent with previous studies on message strategy analysis. Message-based analyses of the phenomenon, including scaling studies to discern perceived severity and descriptive approaches to determine the nature of aggressive and threatening messages, have made a major contribution to our understanding of aggressive communications (Kinney, 1994). A message-based approach is also supportive of the emerging trend in risk management that emphasizes the role of communication. In what is simply referred to as the *threat assessment approach*, "violence is seen as the product of an interaction among the perpetrator, situation, target, and the setting" (Reddy et al., 2001, p. 167). Analyzing multiple interactions and communicative behaviors is expected to provide valuable insight and information concerning the potential for violence.

A number of propositions will guide our work here. These propositions are rooted in communication theory drawn from a discipline framed by a focus on messages, audience, and credibility.[1] They are mentioned here only to frame the analysis and will not be explored in detail.

- Communication behavior is influenced from both cognitive and affective systems.
- Communication behavior can be viewed along a continuum of *planned* to *spontaneous*.
- Communication behavior is contextually driven.
- Communication behavior often involves multiple channels.
- The expressed intent of message strategies is not always executed.
- Risk/threat management requires collaborative effort among stakeholders.
- Risk/threat management is implicated by resource management limitations, first amendment rights, and privacy issues.
- The risk/threat management system is multidisciplinary, contested, and challenged with different nomenclatures.

How individuals process and respond to messages varies according to personal psychological and social perspectives shaped by culture, history, experiences, and circumstances—in other words, according to their *context* (Lewenstein and Brossard, 2006). Because of these demands, communicators must acknowledge, tailor, and execute messages with a number of parameters in mind (O'Hair, 2004; Renn, 2009). Similar to classical rhetorical approaches to message development, the contextual model provides guidance for creating messages relevant to individuals

---

[1] No doubt, many scholars lay claim to the concept of communication as a discipline of study. Our background and the corpora of research pursued in this project are framed primarily from journals sponsored by professional associations whose field of study is communication (e.g., National Communication Association, International Communication Association, Broadcast Education Association, Association for Education in Journalism and Mass Communication).

in specific contexts and groups (Lewenstein, 1992; O'Hair et al., 2010; Wynne, 1995; Ziman, 1992).

Against this backdrop, the areas of communication research that appear most relevant to threatening communications and actions are discussed here. Three areas of communication research that have direct implications for assessing threatening communications and behaviors are addressed. The first area concerns the internal processes of conflict and the behavioral reactions to those internal processes. The second area addresses larger domains of examination, including crisis communication, persuasive communication, and deceptive communication. Next, various modalities and channels that can influence communication and resultant behavior are discussed. Last, future directions for threat assessment are offered.

THE RISE OF CONFLICT

Affect, Cognition, and Emotion in Conflict

Any investigation of human behavior, particularly one that focuses on intense behavioral action, would be remiss if it did not include a discussion of the affective, cognitive, and emotional components that both inform and shape communication and behavior. Although not all threats will be based on conflict, it is likely that some element of conflict is present either when a threat is made or when an individual or a group poses a threat. The body of work pertaining to communication and conflict offers a number of perspectives compatible with threatening communications. Conflict can be described as an expressed struggle between two or more interdependent individuals who perceive incompatible goals (Cahn, 1992). Typically, this struggle becomes more pronouced when the individuals perceive resources to be scarce or when goals are difficult to obtain (Hocker and Wilmot, 1998).

In addition, when individuals have a vested interest in particular goals or attitude objects they may be more likely to experience emotion; consequently, they may also be more likely to engage in conflict. In short, episodes of conflict are typically loaded with negative affect connected to the interruption of goals as well as in response to another person's communicatory reactions. To better understand how conflict plays a role in threatening communications, it is important to discuss the roots of conflict. In addition, considering that many communicators do not explicitly make threats, investigators may want to examine the manifestation of nonverbal signs of conflict.

Daly et al. (1983) categorized emotions based on their affective valence (e.g., pleasant versus unpleasant), level of arousal (e.g., low versus high arousal or passive versus active), and level of intensity (e.g., strong versus weak). In addition, each category can vary in intensity. For example, depression can be considered more intense than sadness; rage can be considered more intense than annoyance. Emotional intensity has been positively associated with increases in physiological changes (Guerrero and La Valley, 2006). Interestingly, a cross-cultural study conducted by Scherer and Wallbott (1994) found the physiological profiles of joy, fear, anger, sadness, shame, and guilt to be similar across 37 different countries. For example, sadness was associated with muscle tension and the feeling of a lump in the throat, whereas joy was associated with an accelerated heartbeat and an increase in temperature. Thus, individuals engaged in conflict are likely to experience physiological changes to the extent that they are emotively aroused. In fact, some level of emotional intensity is needed for interpersonal conflicts because emotional intensity is a motivational factor for engaging in conflict in the first place (Jones, 2000). Indeed, the greater the emotional intensity the more likely an individual may be to engage in conflict with a partner.

The notion that individuals will experience physiological changes when emotively aroused has driven much of the research related to credibility assessment, deception detection, and the interface of technology to identify and demarcate patterns of human communication. Gottman (1994) found that during conflict high emotional intensity is associated with strong levels of physiological changes, such as increased heart rate and blood pressure. Although some individuals may not overtly express threats, individuals who think they are in conflict with a particular person, policy, or agency may show nonverbal signals of conflict-related emotions. Assessments of threatening communications might find research in conflict communication helpful in examining the effects of emotional arousal on threatening communications and ensuing behavior. More specifically, studies might ask what resources are available to ascertain an individual's affective state. Can these tools or techniques be used on large groups or in a very short amount of time? Do current techniques aimed at assessing emotional state take into account the contextual and situational conditions that may increase (or decrease) arousal?

Role of Cognition in Emotion

Although some emotional reaction to conflict may be visceral and largely uncontrollable, people have a tendency to recognize how and why they feel a particular way. The appraisal theory of emotion (Lazarus, 1991) argues that individuals evaluate their emotions in order to make sense or justify their emotions and/or behaviors. Although Lazarus suggests that all negative emotions are alike insofar as they stem from personal goal disruption, and positive emotions stem from goal enhancement or facilitation, appraisals are made at the individual level and are fundamentally evaluative and subjective (Jones, 2000). For example, individuals or groups may have their own understanding or values of what constitutes good or bad, right or wrong, fair or unfair (Guerrero and La Valley, 2006). Judgments of fairness are often highly emotion laden (Planalp, 2003), and anger arises when individuals believe they are treated unfairly or badly (Canary et al., 1998). When individuals are angry because of a perceived or real injustice, they often feel warranted to become aggressive, vengeful, and even violent. In addition, direct expressions of anger have been evaluated favorably if the acts of anger were justifiable (Sereno et al., 1987). For example, families of victims that have been affected by crime often lash out at the accused party formally and informally. This type of behavior would typically not be enacted or accepted without the notion of justifiable anger.

Last, attributions about the source of a conflict have been found to affect communication. Specifically, Sillars (1980) suggests that individuals may alter their communication during a conflict based on three attributions: the cause of the conflict, the intentions or personality traits of the other individual involved in the conflict, and the stability of the conflict. These attributions influence communication, behaviors, and strategies used during a conflict. In addition, individuals have a tendency to make more positive attributions about their own behavior than the behavior of others (Heider, 1958; Langdridge and Butt, 2004; Sillars et al., 2000). Future research should ask whether statements of attribution (about feelings) influence particular strategies of threatening communications and resultant behavior. The value-laden secondary attribution associated with fairness may be a particularly rich area of inquiry. If we can better understand the extent to which individuals associate fairness with both personally and mass-communicated events, the better able we may be to predict particular behaviors and threats associated with judgments of (un)fairness.

Behavioral Reactions to the Elicitation of Emotion

Despite the fact that the link between emotion and behavior has been well studied (cf. Ekman and Davidson, 1994; Lewis and Haviland-Jones, 2000), there remains very little consensus on the exact role emotion plays in specific behaviors. Appraisal theories (Frijda, 1987; Lazarus, 1991) suggest that there are particular action tendencies associated with emotions. Action tendencies are biologically driven coping responses to emotion. Thus, appraisal theory accounts for individual variances of emotional response to the same emotion-eliciting event. Lazarus (1991) offers three characteristics that typically underlie emotion: affect (positive or negative valence), level and type of physiological arousal alteration, and core theme of the emotion-eliciting event. Different emotions are associated with different types of appraisals and action tendencies. For example, the action tendency for anger is to attack, whereas the action tendency for fear is to avoid or move away from harm.

Although these action tendencies are biologically rooted, to a large degree culture may marshal or attenuate affective responses through display rules. For example, a typical action tendency toward anger may be to lash out; however, display rules govern the socially acceptable or socially desired way to display anger. For example, although an employee may become frustrated and angry at work, it is in the employee's best interest to avoid emotional outbursts of anger. Ekman (1978) and Ekman and Friesen (1975) have posited five ways in which individuals manage emotional expression: intensify, deintensify, simulate, inhibit, and mask. Intensification of emotions occurs when individuals act as if they feel more emotion than they actually do. Deintensification of emotion occurs when individuals act as if they feel less emotion than they actually do. Simulation of emotion occurs when individuals act as if they feel an emotion they do not actually feel. Inhibition of emotion occurs when individuals act as if they do not feel an emotion they actually feel. Last, masking of emotion occurs when individuals act as if they feel an emotion that is very different from the emotion actually felt.

These display rules may be used regularly, even to the extent that they are ingratiated beyond active cognition at times. However, during conflict, individuals may find it more difficult to regulate their own emotions (Gottman, 1994). Thus, despite the fact that display rules and socially accepted ways of displaying particular emotions often regulate behavior, when individuals are or believe they are in conflict with a person, an organization, a policy, or a law, for example, they may have less control over how they ultimately display their emotions. Although the idea that individuals who become so overwhelmed with an emotion have a tendency to display that emotion may not be novel, there is not necessarily a correlation between displaying an emotion (e.g., anger) and enacting threatening or violent behavior. In fact, it might be argued that displaying the overwhelming emotion may serve a cathartic purpose for a highly emotive person.

The goal of this section is to further the argument that individuals under affective and emotional distress are likely to communicate this affective and emotional arousal simply because humans are unable to conceal emotional arousal at a physiological level. Future research should assess the specific types of inappropriate or violent behavior most easily predicted from conflict-driven emotions. Although anger may seem to be a natural target of investigations into behavioral outbursts, research into mixed-emotion states may produce a better understanding of the (ir)rational emotion associated with inappropriate behavior. For example, jealousy is a combination of anger and sadness. Individuals who are jealous of nonexistent relationships may lash out at the target of that unrequited relationship or may turn to depressed and self-injurious behaviors. Another example of a mixed emotion is frustration; individuals who are frustrated are likely to produce nonverbal and verbal displays of their emotional arousal. Understanding how stimulus is processed during highly affective states is essential for extrapolating the connection between stimulus, cognitive and emotional appraisals, and future behavior.

Conflict-Related Emotions

Considering the role conflict plays in the elicitation of emotion and the role emotion may play in threatening and violent behavior, we now turn to emotions often associated with conflict. There are several different emotions associated with conflict as well as different activation levels, intensities, and affective valence. The most common emotions relevant to conflict are anger, jealousy, and hurt. Although there are other emotions associated with conflict (e.g., contempt, disgust), this discussion is limited to the most common responses.

Anger

Anger is the first emotion recognized as being associated with conflict. Rage, irritation, exasperation, disgust, and contempt are specific types of emotions associated with anger (Shaver et al., 1987). Angry individuals typically experience accelerated heart rate, tense or tightening muscles, rapid breathing patterns, and a flushed feeling (Scherer and Wallbott, 1994). The greater the intensity of anger the more likely the individual is to become emotionally flooded and have difficulty staying calm and rational (Gottman, 1994). As discussed earlier, one of the major causes of anger can stem from the interruption of one's goals or sense of self-identity.

Canary and colleagues (1998) identified seven possible causes of anger: identity management, aggression, frustration, fairness, incompetence, relationship threat, and predispositions. Anger is a common response when individuals feel as if their identity, public image, or face is being threatened.

Anger is also a common response to aggression, or when an individual is threatened or is actually physically harmed. Frustrating situations include having one's plans interrupted, having an expectation violated negatively, feeling powerless, or experiencing perceptions of injustice. In fact, feelings of unfairness or inequity can cause extreme anger and lead to emotional flooding (Gottman, 1994). In addition, some individuals have a predisposition toward anger, caused by a personality trait, substance abuse, or chemical imbalance.

Anger is typically communicated through the action tendency of attack (Lazarus, 1991). These behaviors may include verbal attacks (discussed later), physical attacks, and nonverbal disapproval (Shaver et al., 1987). However, not all instances of anger result in aggression (Canary et al., 1998). Future research could assess several aspects of anger: How might secondary appraisal processing and the development of coping strategies be implemented to "at-risk" individuals? Could preventative or responsive persuasive messages aimed at disseminating and/or teaching coping strategies be developed?

Jealousy

Jealousy can provide an impetus for threatening behavior. Jealousy can be defined as emotion based on the perceived threat of a relationship by a third party (White and Mullen, 1989). Jealousy can begin as an increase in arousal (Pines and Aronson, 1983) that is typically accompanied by increased heart rate and a feeling of being flushed. Anger and fear are usually central to the emotion of jealousy as well as sadness, guilt, sexual arousal, envy, and love (Guerrero et al., 2005). Jealousy can be communicated in several ways. Guerrero and Andersen (1998) identify several communicative responses to jealousy, including distributive communication (i.e., aggressive and direct forms of communication), active distancing (i.e., aggressive and indirect forms of communication), counterjealousy inductions (i.e., attempts to make another person jealous on purpose), violence toward a partner (e.g., hitting, pushing, grabbing), and violence toward objects (e.g., punching a wall, breaking a vase, tearing a photograph). In addition, jealousy has been associated with conflict styles, such as aggression and completion (Buunk, 1991), and it has been positivity correlated to aggression and violence (Simonelli and Ingram, 1998). Although aggression and violence may be responses to jealousy, nonviolent aggression is also a response to jealous emotions. Often the conflict style and the approach that an individual takes when (not) communicating are as varied as the intensity of the emotion itself.

Hurt

Emotional hurt can best be described as feeling psychologically injured by another person (Vangelisti and Sprague, 1998). Other entities may be able to elicit emotional hurt, too. If the emotion of hurt is triggered by another person's actions, then hurt is fundamentally an interpersonal emotion. However, individuals can experience hurt even if they only perceive to have a relationship with another individual. For example, individuals who obsess, stalk, or only perceive themselves as having a relationship with a particular individual are perfectly capable of feeling emotional hurt. Other emotions that accompany hurt include agony, anger, sadness, and suffering. Although there is no definitive research that has isolated the physiological changes that are brought on by hurt, it is likely that hurt individuals experience anger and sadness. Physiological changes associated with sadness include muscle tension, crying, quietness, and a lump in the throat (Scherer and Wallbott, 1994). Hurtful messages that attack one's personal or relational identity are typical causes of emotional hurt (Vangelisti, 1994). Relational identity can best be described as the values, beliefs, rules, and processes involved in relational maintenance (Wood, 2000). For example, calling someone an idiot is clearly attacking their personal identity; whereas calling someone a horrible mother attacks the personal identity as well as the relational identity because there is a relational expectation for what merits a good mother. Another example would be if an individual found out that a close friend had stolen his or her property; because the theft would violate a relational rule about what it means to be close friends, the individual that had their property stolen would likely experience emotional hurt.

Investigations aimed at understanding threatening and violent communications may want to focus on the emotional hurt an individual is experiencing as well as the emotional hurt that person is trying to inflict by way of threatening messages and communications with potential targets. Vangelisti has identified nine types of hurtful messages: accusations (e.g., statements about one's faults), evaluations (e.g., statements about one's value or worth, often in a negative way), advice (e.g., suggesting a course of action that threatens one's sense of self), expressed desires (e.g., statements about plans that may not include another individual), informative statements (e.g., statements that disclose unflattering facts about another), threats (e.g., to demonstrate an intent to cause harm or injury to another), lies (e.g., statements that obfuscate the truth and may jeopardize a sense of trust), and jokes (e.g., making fun of or teasing someone). Hurtful messages could be caused by or be a consequence of conflict. For example, Infante (1987) suggests that argumentativeness or verbal aggressiveness may be the result of an inability by one party to articulate their point of view or to successfully argue and defend their position.

There are typically three types (Vangelisti and Crumley, 1998) of responses to hurtful messages: active verbal responses (e.g., verbally attacking another person, using sarcasm, asking for an explanation), acquiescence (e.g., crying, conceding, apologizing), and invulnerable responses (e.g., ignoring the hurtful message, laughing at the message, becoming quiet). Thus, when an agency or organization reaches out to a particular individual, it may inadvertently generate a hurtful message. Organizations charged with the task of examining threatening communications may want to also focus on the types of messages they compose, with an emphasis on avoiding hurtful ones. Future research should examine which behaviors are most consistent with threatening communications when motivated by jealousy and hurt feelings. Research that examines the information individuals perceive to be communicated from the target of their fixation would be helpful in determining emotional attachments related to jealousy and hurt feelings.

Additional Areas for Future Research

Much of the research presented in this section approaches emotions and conflict from a rational and linear perspective. Although these findings have been supported, the research conducted thus far may not be particularly illuminating when dealing with irrational and emotionally unstable individuals. For example, although the concepts of emotions and conflict have been discussed in an interpersonal context, it is possible that strangers may experience similar or the same types of emotions associated with a relationship. In fact, stalkers and obsessed individuals may believe they have an interpersonal relationship with someone who is actually a stranger. Although many of the examples may not fit a stalking or an obsessed relationship, these individuals are likely to experience the same physiological changes and display many of the same communication patterns.

More cross-cultural studies need to be conducted in order to make better predictions about how individuals from different cultures deal with emotions and conflict. Ostensibly, culture plays a role in the expression of emotions; however, the extent to which culture alters the process of coping with emotions remains unclear. Scholars have long recognized the importance of investigating the human face. In particular, scholars in nonverbal communication have looked to the face to identify emotional displays in various contexts. Many verbal and nonverbal behaviors are considered to be connected to some degree to affective or emotional responses. For example, there are universal facial expressions that connect closely to different emotions, including fear, anger, sadness, and happiness (Darwin, 1872/1998; Ekman, 1972; Ekman and Friesen, 1971; Ekman et al., 1987).

Prior sections focused on the internal processes of affect, cognition, and emotion related to conflict and discussed physiological changes associated with those processes. Although conflict and related internal processes can produce particular physiological changes, the next section focuses only on the deliberate expression of conflict. Specifically, the section explores verbal aggressiveness and threat assessment.

Giving Voice to Conflict: Verbal Aggressiveness and Threat Assessment

Verbal aggressiveness is an individual's inclination to attack the self-concepts of other people in an effort to cause psychological pain (Infante and Wigley, 1986). This type of aggression, in which a person initiates personal attacks against a select target or victim, is manifested through communication. Not surprisingly, verbal aggressiveness is considered a destructive form of communication (Infante et al., 1992) and an expression of hostility (Martin and Anderson, 1996).

The literature suggests a number of verbally aggressive messages—character attacks, competence attacks, background attacks, physical appearance attacks, cursing, teasing, ridiculing, threats, nonverbal actions, withdrawal, physical acts, rejection, negative affect, and unfair comparisons (Infante et al., 1990; Myers and Bryant, 2008). Kinney (1994) presents a broader typology of verbal aggressiveness, specifically within the context of interpersonal interaction: attacks against group membership, personal failings, and relationship-related failings. Kinnney also suggests a dimensional structure of verbally aggressive messages composed of the (1) target, (2) form of weapon, and (3) force of weapon.

To gain insight into the potential origins of verbal aggressiveness, researchers have studied the phenomenon from various angles, including a trait perspective. Personality traits and natural inclinations to communicate in a particular manner across situations are often referred to as communication predispositions (Rancer and Nicotera, 2007). Acknowledging one's predisposition for aggressive communicatory behavior, Beatty and McCroskey (1997) asserted that "verbal aggressiveness represents expressions of inborn, biological functioning, which is antecedent to social experience" (p. 446). Early on, verbal aggressiveness was associated with hostility (Infante and Wigley, 1986) and argumentative skill deficiency (Infante, 1987). More recently, lack of responsiveness has emerged as a character trait associated with verbal aggressiveness (Martin and Anderson, 1996) and psychoticism (Heisel et al., 2003).

Considering these and potentially other character traits that appear to be associated with verbal aggressiveness may help inform a profiling approach, or even a more exhaustive situational approach, to risk assessment vis-à-vis threatening communications. For example, traits such as hostility, argumentative skill deficiency, and lack of responsiveness may be discovered, revealing useful information about would-be perpetrators of violence.

Over the past 20 years, extensive research has been conducted on the communication trait of verbal aggressiveness. Thus far, approximately 200 articles, convention papers, and dissertations are estimated to have been published (Rancer and Nicotera, 2007). Verbal aggressiveness studies have been conducted primarily in the context of interpersonal communication, specifically marriage and family interactions, and organizational communication (Infante and Rancer, 1996). Other relevant contexts include educational communication (e.g., Kearney et al., 1991; McPherson et al., 2003; Avtgis and Rancer, 2008), mass media communication (e.g., Sebastian et al., 1978), and intercultural communication (e.g., Prunty et al., 1990; Suzuki and Rancer, 1994).

Research on verbal aggressiveness has often been partnered with studies in another related dimension of aggressive communication—argumentativeness. Unlike verbal aggressiveness, argumentativeness is widely considered a constructive, rather than destructive, form of communication that is related to positive relational outcomes (Infante and Rancer, 1982). Examples include increased perceived credibility (Infante, 1985) and relationship satisfaction (Sabourin et al., 1993). Argumentativeness has been defined as "a generally stable trait which predisposes the individual in communication situations to advocate positions on controversial issues and to attack verbally the positions which other people take on these issues" (Infante and Rancer, 1982, p. 72). Thus, the target of attack is the primary distinguishing factor between verbal aggressiveness and argumentativeness. A person's self-concept is the target for verbal aggressiveness, and a person's position on an issue is the locus of attack for argumentativeness (Infante et al., 1989). Future research might consider to what extent verbal aggressiveness and threatening communications share verbal characteristics.

Other interesting findings have also differentiated the two dimensions of aggressive communications. First, highly argumentative individuals are more varied in their communication strategies so as to gain compliance, whereas verbally aggressive individuals maintain a consistent approach rather than diversify their strategy selection (Boster et al., 1993). Second, argumentativeness is perceived to increase a person's credibility, whereas verbal aggressiveness reduces credibility (Infante and Rancer, 1996). Third, argumentative individuals are naturally skilled in argumentation, but verbally aggressive individuals lack proficiency in argumentation abilities, an observation addressed in the argumentation skill deficiency model of Infante et al. (1989). Although argumentativeness and verbal aggressiveness are related conceptually, research indicates a clear distinction between the two dimensions of aggressive communication. Therefore, future research might ask if verbal aggressiveness and argumentativeness can be used as predictors of threatening communication and violent behavior.

Most of the interesting findings from the literature are too numerous to discuss here, but at least one finding is noteworthy and may have relevance to threat and risk assessment. For some time, verbal aggressiveness has been described as a catalyst to physical violence (Infante et al., 1989; Infante and Rancer, 1996). It has been suggested, especially in various interpersonal communication contexts, that "verbal aggressiveness sometimes escalates into physical violence" (Infante and Wigley, 1986, p. 62). Specifically, negative relationship outcomes have been associated with an individual's predisposition for verbal aggressiveness, including physical aggression, abuse, and violence (Rogan and La France, 2003). Interestingly, individuals who lack communication skills such as argumentativeness, which is necessary for effective conflict resolution, have a tendency to demonstrate verbally aggressive behavior that results in violent behavior (Infante et al., 1989). When an individual thinks he/she has reached the end of his/her abilities to argue, rationalize, or express him- or herself effectively, verbal aggressiveness may result, which may lead to subsequent physical violence. This observation supports Deturck's (1987) claim that, when communication attempts fail, physical aggression is used to gain compliance. Future research could delve deeper to ask how verbal aggressiveness, threatening communication, and physical behavior are sequenced. Does verbal aggressiveness lead to threats such that a communicator would feel obligated to carry them out?

As studies in verbal aggressiveness have evolved over the past 20 years, research has acknowledged the distinctiveness of this form of aggression and shifted to a more narrow focus. Once treated mainly as one of many types of aggressive behavior, verbal aggressiveness is now being isolated to better understand its unique attributes. To assist in such a direct approach, Infante and Wigley (1986) developed a *verbal aggressiveness scale*, which emerged from an interpersonal model of aggression and includes concepts such as argumentativeness. Factor analysis and item analysis on the initial scale, using 30 items, resulted in a 20-item unidimensional scale with 10 positively worded items and 10 negatively worded items. Initial studies and subsequent research have found evidence of the validity of the measure, with an alpha coefficient of at least .81 (Infante and Wigley, 1986; Boster et al., 1993).

More recent studies have further developed the verbal aggressiveness scale, suggesting bidimensionality of the measure. The 10 negatively worded, or "aggressively worded," items appear to more accurately measure verbal aggressiveness, whereas the positively worded items seem to measure a more pro-social, confirming communication style (Levine et al., 2004). The authors suggested reducing the scale to the 10 aggressively worded items to obtain a more accurate reflection of verbal aggressiveness.

Risk assessment within interpersonal interactions, namely dyadic and family relations, has been informed by studies in verbal aggressiveness and use of the verbal aggressiveness scale. Because "verbal aggression sometimes escalates into physical violence" (Infante and Wigley, 1986, p. 62), a useful measure of the concept provides insight into potential violence. However, use of the scale in the context of risk assessment of threatening communications is seemingly nonexistent. As previously mentioned, verbal aggressiveness is considered a personality trait emerging from an individual's predisposition to communicate aggressively (Infante and Wigley, 1986; Beatty and McCroskey, 1997). Moreover, one of the major challenges facing risk assessment approaches is understanding the character of the person posing a threat and his or her potential level of danger (Smith, 2008a). Use of the verbal aggressiveness scale is expected to provide some level of insight into the character of the threatener and the potential for violent behavior.

The obvious limitation inherent in such an approach is the feasibility and probability of getting a would-be perpetrator to complete the scale. Previous studies have successfully modified the scale by making it functional and reliable as an observational measure. Spouses have used the scale to report the verbally aggressive nature of their partners (Infante et al., 1989), and third-party observers have used a modified version of the scale to measure the verbal aggressiveness of others (Heisel et al., 2003). These adaptations of the scale to use in observational contexts may prove beneficial for efforts in threat assessment. Examiners can potentially use an adapted scale to measure the verbally aggressive nature of those who make threats, providing insight into their character. Of course, observational information can only be gathered on potential perpetrators if data exist. Online profile information available on social networking sites, blogs, and messages boards, threatening messages, and other personal information collected through investigation are likely sources of such information. Future research should validate the observational format of the verbal aggressiveness scale (metrics) for the threat behavior context.

Verbal aggressiveness has relevance to risk and threat assessment efforts for two primary reasons. First, verbal aggressiveness has been linked to physical violence. From the onset, threat of physical attack, in which someone communicates intent to inflict physical harm on another individual, has been considered a dimension of verbal aggressiveness (Greenberg, 1976). Subsequent studies posited verbal aggressiveness as a *catalyst* to violence when certain situational factors are present and active (Infante et al., 1989). Especially in the context of marriage and family interactions, aggressive communication has been shown to trigger physical violence. Specifically, character attacks, swearing, competence attacks, and threats have been shown to facilitate physical violence (Infante et al., 1990). Negative outcomes such as physical aggression, abuse, and violence seemingly result from little or no concern for the targeted individual, a common phenomenon for verbally aggressive individuals (Rogan and La France, 2003). Because verbal aggressiveness is a subset of hostility and is so closely linked to physical violence, it is expected to inform risk and threat assessment efforts by law enforcement and others.

A second reason verbal aggressiveness has application value in the context of threat assessment is that a situational approach to risk management should consider the nature and character of the would-be perpetrator. Verbal aggressiveness has been described from a trait perspective, suggesting something specific about the character and nature of the attacker. Caprara and Pastorelli (1989) used a personality perspective to develop a measure of a person's propensity for violence. Profiling approaches that analyze the type of individual making threats, along with guided judgment and automated decision making, are traditional forms of risk assessment (Reddy et al., 2001). More recently, a more expansive and deductive approach that considers multiple situational factors has been used. Research supports such a situational threat assessment approach "because a knowledge of individual differences will allow future theory to specify how characteristics of the situation and attributes of the person interact to produce behavior" (Infante et al., 1992, p. 117). Understandably, even within a contextual and situational approach to threat assessment, the character of the individual making the threat should be examined. Thus, verbal aggressiveness may provide at least one contextual clue or situational factor in the risk assessment process.

Although research on the link between verbal aggressiveness and future violent behavior could provide promise for risk assessment development, there are some limitations to this line of research. Although several studies have investigated the role of verbal aggressiveness in future violent behaviors, these studies rely on self-reported data, which can be overtly biased by social desirability, fallacious memory, and self-interests. Another limitation concerns the relationship between verbal aggression and violence or physical aggression as a *response* behavior provoked by someone else's verbal aggressiveness rather than a successive behavior after one's own verbally aggressive communication. For example, Goldstein and Rosenbaum (1985) examined how verbal aggressiveness in the form of character attacks reinforced negative self-image and became a catalyst for physical violence. Spouses felt like their self-esteem was being attacked (i.e., verbal aggressiveness) and therefore reacted with physical aggression toward their partners. Furthermore, recent research has called into question the validity of the verbal aggression construct. Kotowski et al. (2009) argue that the verbal aggressiveness scale actually measures two constructs: verbal aggressiveness and verbal benevolence communication style. In addition, they report that the scale is unidimensional with several poor items. In fact, their multimethod data found near zero correlations between self-reports and observed behavior. Thus, these researchers argue that there is a discrepancy between the conceptual definitions of verbal aggressiveness and behaviors.

Although recent research has called into question the current constructs used to measure verbal aggressiveness, understanding the link between verbal aggressiveness and future violent behaviors would seemingly advance the body of knowledge of both verbal aggressiveness and risk assessment. Is it possible for physical violence to occur not just as a response to verbal aggressiveness in a communicative dyad but as a natural subsequent behavior to one's own verbal aggressiveness? In other words, are verbal aggressiveness and physical aggression positively related on the individual level? If so, the existence of verbal aggressiveness as a character trait of threateners may provide useful information into the potential for violence in a threatening situation.

The previous section addressed the verbal expression of emotion. In particular, the section explored the decades of research on verbal aggressiveness and future violent behavior. Recently, a great body of work has amassed around a burgeoning area of research specifically focused on risk and crisis communication. Although this research is still emerging, many of the conclusions are based on case studies and actual crisis or hostage scenarios. Thus, understanding communications between a perpetrator of threats or violence and larger organizations may be useful in research to assess threatening communications and behavior.

CRISIS COMMUNICATION

The emerging field of crisis/hostage negotiation represents one of the most critical and complex areas of human interaction (Rogan and Hammer, 2006). In particular, crisis/hostage negotiation deals with the interaction between effective communication and saving human lives. As such, crisis/hostage negotiation research has theoretical and pragmatic applications for threatening communications. Communication-based research on crisis/hostage negotiation is a relatively new area of inquiry. Much of this research orients around discourse/content analysis of transcribed recordings of actual hostage-taking incidents (Rogan and Hammer, 2006).

Relational Interdependence

Drawing on the work of Snyder and Diesing (1977), Donohue et al. (1991a, 1991b) have led the way in relational interdependence in crisis negotiation. Relational interdependence can best be described as a reciprocal relation of mutual dependence or influence between two individuals. They have suggested that features of crisis and hostage negotiation increase emotional intensity, thereby increasing the pressures on law enforcement personnel, particularly when a crisis/hostage negotiator is trying to establish a relationship with a suspect. Additionally, the core relational issues of control and distance create a double bind, or paradox, in which both negotiator and suspect attempt to gain control of the conversation and either sustain a coercive interdependence between one another or move toward a cooperative and normative barraging relationship.

This notion of a double bind was further explored in examining the immediacy behaviors of negotiators and suspects. Donohue et al. have defined immediacy as directness and intensity of communication and have also differentiated between implicit immediacy (openness about one's thoughts, feelings, and needs) and spatial immediacy (communication that conveys physical and psychological closeness). In their examination of nine actual hostage negotiations, they found that incidents involving mentally ill suspects typically started as cooperative and became increasingly more competitive, whereas incidents involving criminals typically began as competitive and became increasingly more cooperative. Domestic incidents remained competitive throughout the negotiations.

This paradox was examined furthered by Donohue and Roberto (1993). They identified four limits of the interaction of relational affiliation and relational interdependence: (1) moving toward the other party, (2) moving away from the other party, (3) moving with the other party, and (4) moving against the other party. Donohue and Roberto discovered that stable relational dynamics were established fairly early in the negotiations and that both parties typically adhered to this structure. Moving-away and moving-against behaviors were typically marked by an inability to establish relational understanding, whereas moving-toward and moving-with patterns of behavior were consistent with enhanced relational consensus. In short, Donohue and Roberto offered negotiated-order theory as a framework to understand the implicit communication dynamics that both suspects and negotiators experience as they draw boundaries around their relationships and ultimately determine the outcome of a crisis/hostage incident. Future studies should investigate how relational interdependence dimensions can be integrated into analyses of threatening communications.

Behavioral Model of Crisis Negotiation

Research by Hammer and Rogan has focused on the communication-based components of crisis negotiation (Hammer and Rogan, 1997; Rogan and Hammer, 1994, 1995, 2002; Rogan et al., 1997a, 1997b). They posit a four-part behavioral model based on the communicative dynamics of crisis negotiation, labeled S.A.F.E. The model consists of four interpretive frames: substantive demands/wants, attunement, face, and emotional distress. A substantive frame refers to an individual concern for generally objective and tangible wants and demands (Roloff and Jordan, 1992). During crisis negotiations, typically two types of substantive goals are identified: central and peripheral substantive interests/demands (Hammer and Rogan, 1997; Rogan and Hammer, 2002). Central substantive interests and demands involve situation-related wants; peripheral interests and demands are not specific to the situation. For example, a request for transportation away from a crisis incident would be considered a central substantive demand, whereas a request for food or water would communicate a peripheral substantive demand.

Hammer (2001) suggests that the amount and type of interests and demands communicated during a crisis negotiation are related to escalation or de-escalation of an incident. For example, increased communication of peripheral demands and greater commitment to previously communicated peripheral demands denotes an increase in escalation. However, a tendency to communicate more central substantive demands and a reduction in peripheral substantive demands denotes a de-escalation of the crisis incident.

Attunement relates to the negotiation of relational dynamics between subject and negotiator (Rogan and Hammer, 2002). For example, trust, affiliation, power, and understanding are all considered components of personal relationships. Typically, a negotiator must work toward establishing many of these components with a subject. In fact, many negotiations often begin by attempting to establish some sort of trust in the relationship. The importance of developing a positive relationship between subject and negotiator is considered essential to incident resolution. In addition, Donohue and Roberto (1993) contend that the level of relational distance (attunement) between subjects and negotiators communicates attraction, liking, respect, trust, and willingness to cooperate.

Face can best be described as an individual concern for self, image maintenance reputation, and/or identity that is presented during a social interaction (Hammer and Rogan, 1997; Ting-Toomey and Kurogi, 1998). Rogan and Hammer (1994) suggest that in crisis negotiation context, face varies across three dimensions: locus of concern (self or other directed), face valence (defend, maintain, attack, or honor face), and temporality (attempts to protect against loss of face or efforts to restore face). Applying these conceptions of face to three actual crisis negotiation incidents, these authors found that crisis negotiators were more likely to engage in efforts to restore other's face and that suspects were more likely to engage in restoring self-face or attacking self-face. Self-face refers to one's own presentation and maintenance of face. Conversely, other face is the presentation and maintenance of other individuals' face. In addition, Rogan and Hammer suggest that two other types of face are of particular importance in crisis negotiation: group identity and individual identity. These authors conclude that personal identity may be more likely in negotiations that involve suicide; social identity is more common in incidents involving members of particular groups, cults, or national organizations.

Emotional distress is often a key indicator of success or failure in crisis negotiation. Negotiators are typically trained to listen and respond to a subject's emotions in order to mitigate the potential for a negative and/or violent behavior. Essentially the belief is that, if the negotiator can calm the suspect, it is more likely the suspect will return to rational and normative bargaining. In a study investigating the verbal expression of emotion in actual crisis negotiations, emotions were intense and very negative at the outset of the interaction (Rogan and Hammer, 1995). Subjects typically became more positive as the negotiation proceeded through various stages. However, in incidents in which the suspect committed suicide, emotions remained intense and negative throughout the interaction. This line of research offers a preliminary glance at emotional expression during crisis negotiation and presents a direction for future research regarding the need to fully understand an individual's emotional state, as it may forecast future behavior (Rogan and Hammer, 2006).

Although most negotiators are trained to access the emotional state of a suspect, a law enforcement agent often only has a line of questioning, paraphrasing, and emotional labeling in order to make this assessment (Rogan and Hammer, 2006). Therefore, this paper addresses some of the complexities involved in emotional states and behavioral outcomes. For example, emotion is likely the outcome of cognitive appraisal processes, influenced by social and cultural aspects, and is linked to discrete and indiscriminate psychological and physiological experiences, which combine to generate some sort of emotional expression (Izard, 1990). Rogan and Hammer (1995), however, investigated language-based affective messages by examining a suspect's verbal communication and found preliminary patterns associated with communication and the suspect's violent and suicidal behavior. Thus, future research should continue to explore the relationship between emotional appraisal and verbal and nonverbal communication patterns of predictive behavioral outcomes.

PERSUASION AND THREATENING BEHAVIORS

Smith (2008a) discovered a relationship between persuasive communication used in threatening messages and the likelihood of acting on a threat. Obviously, persuasion and other forms of social influence represent general categories of research that refer to attempts at attitude and behavioral change. It comes as no surprise that threatening communications would be linked to persuasion attempts. Given the vast body of work on persuasion and social influence, it would not be productive to review here the numerous studies in this area. Instead, the focus is on a subset of persuasion research studies that seem most likely to yield promising results as a comparative area of investigation for threatening behavior—fear appeals.

Fear Appeals

There has been nearly 50 years of research on fear appeals in various disciplines, and these studies have collectively garnered mixed results (for an overview, see Ruiter et al., 2001). However, fear appeals are commonly used to modify behavior. Fear appeals are persuasive messages designed to scare or frighten people into complying with a particular message by describing the awful and terrible things that will happen to them if they do not act in accordance with the message (Witte, 1992a). Fear itself can best be understood as an emotion with negative valence accompanied by a high level of arousal that is perceived to be both significant and personally relevant and that motivates people to action (Easterling and Leventhal, 1989; Frijda, 1986; Ortony and Turner, 1990; Witte, 1992b, 1998).

Parallel Response Model

The parallel response model suggests that fear appeals generate two separate processes: danger control and fear control. Danger control processes involve attempts to control the danger or threat; fear control processes involve attempts to control one's own fear generated by the danger or threat. When people are motivated to control a danger, they typically think about the fear appeal and of ways to remove or lessen the threat. Typically, they think carefully about the recommended responses advocated in the persuasive message and attempt to adopt those as a means to control the danger. On the other hand, when people are motivated to control their fear, they can no longer think about the fear appeal or the danger of the threat; instead, they focus on how frightened they feel and they attempt to get rid of their fear through denial, defensive avoidance, or reactance.

Witte and Allen's (2000) Extended Parallel Process Model (EPPM), which traces its lineage through the classic fear-appeal theories, attempts to explain both when and why fear appeals work, as well as when and why they fail. According to EPPM, if a threat is perceived as irrelevant or insignificant, there is little motivation to process the message further. Conversely, when the threat is perceived or believed to be serious and relevant, individuals become afraid and are motivated to act in order to reduce their fear. The EPPM suggests that in some cases fear-arousing messages can lead to danger control processes, which in turn generate adaptive potentially life-saving actions. In other cases, fear-arousing messages can lead to fear-controlling processes, which can lead to maladaptive and potentially life-threatening actions. Lastly, EPPM emphasizes the role self-efficacy plays in the type of control process a person chooses. Specifically, the model suggests that people must be self-efficacious in order to maximize their danger-controlling processes in response to fear-arousing messages. Future research should assess whether threatening messages are more likely to lead to threatening behavior if they contain elements of fear (danger) control and self-efficacy. Research efforts could subsequently assess how messages aimed at curbing unwanted behaviors (e.g., sending letters, making threats) might incorporate enough fear and efficacy to promote behavioral changes.

Generally, for fear appeals to be effective, they should include three key factors: use a credible source, relate to a receiver's self-esteem, and focus on an important topic (Pfau and Parrot, 1993). Hale and Dillard (1995) echo the advice of Pfau and Parrot and offer several of their own suggestions for designing fear-appeal messages for optimal effectiveness. First, Hale and Dillard suggest the need for a threat component; in other words, the fear-appeal message must arouse the emotion of fear. To accomplish a sufficient threat component, a fear-appeal message must include a threat of severe physical or social harm if the recipient of the message does not comply with the recommendations. In addition, a fear appeal should personalize the risk to the target of the message. In other words, the recipient of the message must feel vulnerable or susceptible to the threat and to the consequences of not following the recommendations.

An effective fear appeal should also contain an action component; there are two primary types of action components: personal efficacy and response efficacy (Hale and Dillard, 1995; Stephenson and Witte, 2001; Witte, 1992a). Personal efficacy refers to the target's perception of whether he or she can actually engage in the recommendations provided in the message. In contrast, response efficacy concerns whether the recommendations offered by the message are effective at eliminating or reducing the threat depicted. Thus, a successful fear-appeal message must ensure that the effectiveness of the recommended response is clearly demonstrated within the message (Hale and Dillard, 1995). Threatening messages should be examined for levels of personal and response efficacy and to determine their effect on ensuring specific behavior.

Additional concerns include organization of the message, vividness of the message, framing of the message, whether the target is a volunteer, age of the target(s), anxiety of the target(s), and the cost of responding to the recommendations (Hale and Dillard, 1995). Although there are several ways to arrange a fear-appeal message (topical, cause-effect, problem-solution), Hale and Dillard recommend organizing the message using the problem-solution pattern because it is typically easy to follow and well suited to incorporating the aforementioned recommendations (e.g., severe threat, personal and response efficacy). Similar to fear-appeal research, threatening messages should be evaluated to determine if they are more likely to be executed if they follow a problem-solution organizational pattern.

Agencies and organizations interested in using persuasive messages to deter threatening communications and violent behavior can utilize a fear-appeal strategy to shift a would-be attacker's attitudes. Specifically, these persuasive messages can focus on creating messages that instill fear and efficacy to incorporate the suggestions of the persuasive message to limit or stop threatening messages and possible escalation to violent behavior. Additionally, future research could investigate the extent to which a threatening behavior is an attempt to generate a fear-appeal response and thus effectively respond to communications within the fear-appeal model.

DECEPTIVE COMMUNICATION

For a number of years work in deception and its detection has been the focus of inquiry by researchers, with some encouraging results (Bond and DePaulo, 2006; Burgoon and Qin, 2006; DePaulo et al., 2003; Meservy et al., 2005; Vrij, 2000). According to Burgoon and Varadan (2006): Deception detection is an essential part of investigations involving terrorism and espionage, such as the Hanssen FBI spy case (Havill, 2001). Follow-on asssessment of the Hanssen case identified cues to deception in electronic messages that could have proven successful in detecting his deception had they only been employed for that purpose (Burgoon and Varandan, 2006). A great deal of the work in deception and detection that is related to threatening behavior has focused on behavioral observation and drawing conclusions about veracity and credibility (Burgoon et al., 2005; Pollina, et al., 2006).

The deception detection literature appears to have implications for the study of threatening communications and ensuing behavior. Both systems of communication involve strategies that pose escalating risks to the communicator, depending on the reaction of the target or third parties. Both strategies are likely to carry with them elevated levels of affective arousal, making them more susceptible to certain types of detection or marking (see below). And both strategies are likely to be communicated under conditions varying from predatory to spontaneous. Given the similarities in tactical and strategic features of threatening messages and deception, it would be advantageous to develop studies comparing these systems for their commonalities, making extrapolation of the more extant deception research available to scientists who focus on threatening communications. Likewise, deception researchers would benefit from other researchers' studies of threatening messages. The body of work known as deception research is at an important crossroads given the emergence of new methods and technology that can be applied to studies of detecting credible communications (Burgoon et al., 2008; Burgoon and Varadan, 2006).

Channels of nonverbal communication that have been amenable to analysis in the past include vocalics (or paralanguage), which pertains to human vocalizations; proxemics, a category for distancing and spacing patterns among humans; and kinesics, which categorizes forms of body movement, including facial, gestural, postural, and gait. Unfortunately, isolated behaviors from linguistic, visual, vocal, or other nonverbal behaviors have seldom proven reliable 100 percent of the time. In fact, deception detection accuracy rarely exceeds chance levels. Some of the more promising strategies for distinguishing deceit from truth are in methods that utilize configurations of cues. If computer-assisted detection tools can be developed to support human detection capabilities by discerning micromomentary features of language and nonverbal behavior and by tracking these cues over time, accuracy in discerning both truthful and deceptive information and communications could be substantially improved (Burgoon et al., 2008).

Another strategy intended to increase accuracy is that of distinguishing truthful information from deceptive information in a near-real-time environment. This requires precise instrumentation for dynamic computer-assisted analysis of communication streams. Messages could be captured as analog recordings or with tape-based digital instruments that must then be compressed and edited before they can be coded and analyzed serially. Burgoon et al. (2008) suggest that "many vocal and motion-oriented deception cues are elusive and warrant deployment of more elaborate means of measurement than traditionally used. Daily advances in digital technology are increasing the fidelity, ease, automaticity, and simultaneity of behavioral data capture, which could greatly accelerate the processes of coding and analyzing deceptive messages and could record audio and visual behavior at a fidelity that can be used to develop algorithms for more accurate, automated behavioral analysis" (p. 6). Future research might ask how computer-assisted deception detection tools could be incorporated into studies of threatening and violent behavior. Are these computer-assisted tools and techniques portable and easily disseminated? How might culture attenuate or accentuate verbal and nonverbal displays of deception?

Physiological monitoring can be accomplished through remote sensing technologies. Associated markers include heart and respiration rates, blood flow, electrodermal responses, electroencephalograph changes, eye movement, pupil movement and dilation, micromuscle tremors in the voice and face (O'Hair and Cody, 1987), and other neurophysiological responses—using either contact-based or noncontact measurement devices that may be combined. Given the arousal-laden context of threatening communications, in the future, remote sensing technology might be applied from deception research to the context of threatening communications.

As mentioned above, there is no single behavioral indicator that is known to reliably signal deception or intention on its own. Deception and intention often manifest themselves in many facets of human behavior, including visual phenomena (such as facial expression, gaze direction variation, and gesture), audio phenomena (such as vocal pitch and longer response latency), and physiological phenomena (such as autonomic arousal, as indicated by pupil dilation; DePaulo et al., 2003; Ekman, 2001; O'Hair and Cody, 1994; Zuckerman and Driver, 1985). Multimodal approaches to the detection of deception and hostile intention are likely to prove most powerful. Additional research would be needed to identify which potential indicators of threatening communications (as implicated from deception cues) can be combined to index a more accurate assessment of resultant violent behavior from threatening messages.

Although there are multiple strategies available to detect deception, recent research has called into question the methods used to assess detection deception accuracy (cf. Pigott and Wu, 2008). Some research has demonstrated the usefulness of strategic evidence disclosure. For example, Hartwig et al. (2005) examined the timing of evidence disclosure as a deception detection tool and found that the strategic disclosure of evidence was beneficial for pinpointing lies. In addition, Hartwig et al. (2006) trained interviewers to apply different strategies of evidence disclosure. They found a considerably higher deception detection accuracy rate (85 percent) compared to untrained interviewers (56 percent).

MODALITIES AND CHANNELS

Channel Selection Theories

Those who threaten others have a number of communication channels available to them—social networks, texting, and phone calls. Channel selection is sometimes a spontaneous and convenient choice, whereas in cases of predation the choice of channel can be quite strategic. Selection of a channel for communicating is a critical factor in determining the levels of receptivity or resistance to the information being communicated. Through a comprehensive survey, Trevino et al. (2000) used multiple communication theories to study media attitudes and behaviors. Their results suggested that objective, social, and person/technology factors such as perceived media richness, message equivocality, number of recipients, perceived recipients' attitudes, and distance between message sender and receiver all had merit for explaining media attitudes and behaviors.

Media richness refers to a communication channel's ability to convey a range of visual, auditory, and verbal cues to a receiver (Daft and Lengel, 1984; Kraut et al., 1992). Based on this theory, it may be possible to determine how communication cues (and the nature of such cues) influence threateners' use of different channels in sending and acting on threats. The main premise of media richness theory is that the richness of the medium should match the requirements of the message. Each type of communication has characteristics that make it more appropriate for certain situations and less so for others (Lengel and Daft, 1988). Carlson and Davis (1998) state that, "While many activities are involved in communication, one that is of particular importance is media selection" (p. 335). This thought is also found in research from Zmud et al. (1990): "Communication channels are believed to vary in their capacity to promote rich communication" (p. 440). A rich communication medium has potential for instant feedback, both verbal and nonverbal cues are present, natural language is used, and the focus is on individuals rather than a large group (Zmud et al., 1990).

Lengel and Daft (1988) explain the richness hierarchy by stating the following: "Face-to-face is the richest medium because it has the capacity for direct experience, multiple information cues. . . . Telephone conversations and interactive electronic media provide rapid feedback, but lack the element of 'being there'. . . . Written media . . . such as memos, notes, and reports, can be personally focused but they convey limited cues. . . . Impersonal written media (including fliers, bulletins, and standard computer reports) are the leanest, providing no personal focus on a single receiver. . . . Thus, each medium has an information capacity based on its ability to facilitate multiple cues, feedback, and personal focus" (p. 226). Fulk and Collins-Jarvis (2001) describe simple, predictable tasks with low uncertainty surrounding their message as examples of communication that can be conveyed indirectly. Under high task uncertainty and under conditions of equivocality (that is, multiple possible meanings exist) (Daft and Lengel, 1984; Weick, 1979), it has been shown that direct, straightforward communication is required. "A key premise is that the complexity of communication and information processing mechanisms (e.g., rules vs. meetings) should match the uncertainty inherent in the task itself" (Fulk and Collins-Jarvis, 2001, p. 628).

Katz and Rice (2002) discuss propositions that have applicability in an organizational communication context: "The telephone allows intense immediacy. . . . Transmission of both information and affect [is] highly important, and users may be extraordinarily sensitive to nuances, regardless of the medium. . . . Use of telecommunication technology leaves important residues that reveal complex communicative interactions. . . . Users can be highly creative in developing ad hoc solutions and crossing media boundaries" (pp. 247-252). Two questions could be asked in future research: (1) Are threats communicated through rich media more likely to lead to resultant behavior? (2) Is multiple channel use more likely to signal a threat-behavior connection than single channel use?

Online Communication

The Internet has become the engine that drives many sources of new media, such as online videos, blogs, streaming radio, and instant messaging. What is notable about these new media sources is the lack of regulation relative to traditional sources, such as television, radio, and newspapers (Heath and O'Hair, 2009; Matusitz and O'Hair, 2008). Anyone with access to the Internet can create a website to deliver messages to a target group, gather material from a variety of sources, and interact with other like-minded individuals in synchronous or asynchronous formats. Given the broad audience and relative ease of dissemination, these new media sources are fertile ground for the proliferation of threatening messages (Allen et al., 2009; Matusitz and O'Hair, 2008). Ideological individuals and groups can be defined as those with strongly held values that form a mental model for how they interpret events in the world (Mumford et al., 2008). At the most extreme, such individuals and groups can have antisocial or even violent worldviews. In the case of violent ideological groups, one goal may be to draw in people who are disenchanted and therefore vulnerable to the violent ideology being offered (e.g., Blazak 2001; Moghaddam, 2005).

The motivation for media use typically concerns attainment of various interactive and informational needs, depending on the availability, and the instrumentality of the media to meet these needs (e.g., Rubin,

1993, 1994). Papacharissi and Rubin (2000) discovered that individuals who were less satisfied with life and who felt less socially valued were more likely to use the Internet to facilitate interpersonal communication. These motivations and characteristics are some examples of the psychological needs that resonate with characteristics of ideological groups or a group's members. Violent groups may have more malevolent reasons for being drawn to the new media, and research demonstrates that the new media can be used for cyberterrorism (Matusitz and O'Hair, 2008; Stanton, 2002), intimidation (Corman and Schiefelbein, 2006), and written attacks (Damphousse and Smith, 2002). Stanton (2002) describes a scenario in which intelligent programs, or bots, are used by terrorist groups to interact with users and spread propaganda online. In general, it can be concluded from this research that a variety of communication needs in conjunction with social and situational characteristics can interact with media characteristics to determine media choice and use.

Websites are often described in terms of interactivity. Jensen (1998) is a central proponent of interactivity and casts it as the ability of a medium to allow user influence on the content of the mediated communication. In a similar fashion, Dholakia et al. (2000) argues that interactive websites are those that stimulate perceptions of social presence and are facilitated through reciprocal communication. According to this perspective, user control, responsiveness, connectedness, and playfulness are key criteria for encouraging interactivity. The interactionist perspective (empathy between object, perceiver, and communicator) has been compared to other communication and psychological concepts such as "mirroring," "persuasiveness," the "matching hypothesis," and the "similarity-attraction" paradigm (Moss et al., 2007).

The field of marketing communication research takes a more technical approach to interactivity and website properties, arguing for more focused attention on two-way communication, navigability (lower information search costs), multimedia design (link, graphics, visuals, sounds), and marketing content (company-related information, customer-related information exchange; Karayanni and Baltas, 2003). Song and Zinkhan (2008) investigated the direct effects of interactivity on perceived website effectiveness by operationalizing dimensions of interactivity theory (Rafaeli, 1988) and telepresence theory (Steuer, 1992). Their findings suggest that interactivity perceptions (personalized communication, control, responsiveness) resonate with website users, especially under conditions when cognitive control is elevated. But one question needs to be asked: What dimensions of online communication are most conducive to threatening behavior?

A frequently reported dimension of interactivity is *interaction efficacy*, which can be described as the extent to which people feel comfortable talking to others online and how real time the communication seems (Sohn and Lee, 2005). This is sometimes called synchronicity (e.g., Morris and Ogan, 1996; Porter, 2004). Certain forms of Web communication are more conducive to information exchange; others are more appropriate for social interaction (Maclaran and Catterall, 2002). For example, message boards are more conducive to information exchange (a more asynchronous form of communication), whereas chat rooms are more conducive to social interaction (a more synchronous form of communication). If violent ideological individuals and groups are presumed to be more likely to emphasize community building than nonviolent people, it may also be presumed that these individuals will seek more interaction efficacy in their websites. Higher interaction efficacy facilitates community building through participation in more "real" dialogue than in more asynchronous forms of communication. This will also allow group members to form more personal relationships with others. Along these lines, future research could study whether threats and advocated violent behaviors are more likely to occur on online venues that offer more interactional efficacy.

Online Communication Metrics

As a means of summarizing some of the relevant research focused on online communication, Table 2-1 identifies measures and metrics that have either been used in online communication research or have been suggested as worthy candidates for inclusion in future areas of experimental or case study research. Particular metrics used in online research are identified, followed by a description, a purpose, or an objective for the metric. For each metric an associated marker, outcomes expected from using the metric, and short explanations for the metric's relevance to other types of online analyses are provided.

FUTURE OF THREAT ASSESSMENT

> Threatening situations are more likely to be successfully investigated and managed if other agencies and systems—both within and outside law enforcement or security organizations—are recognized and used to help solve problems presented by a given case. Examples of such systems are those employed by prosecutors; courts; probation, corrections, social service, and mental health agencies; employee assistance programs; victims' assistance programs; and community groups. (Fein et al., 1995, p. 3)

This section supports many arguments laid out by Meloy and colleagues (Biesterfeld and Meloy, 2008; Meloy et al., 2008) and develops arguments for a more integrated and cooperative approach to threat assessment. Communication-related processes such as collaboration and boundary spanning are introduced to frame a strategy for threat assessment systems.

A General Accounting Office report (Posner, 2002) was highly critical of the previous collaboration efforts by various organizations involved in terrorism management:

> Our previous work has found fragmentation and overlap among federal (terrorism) assistance programs. Over 40 federal entities have roles in combating terrorism, and past federal efforts have resulted in a lack of accountability, a lack of a cohesive effort, and duplication of programs. As state and local officials have noted, this situation has led to confusion, making it difficult to identify available federal preparedness resources and effectively partner with the federal government. (p. 3)

Hadden (1989) suggests that institutional barriers often prevent reliable and comprehensive data analysis. Such barriers result, at least in part, from statutes that do not specify which technical data are crucial and therefore should be collected. Required to provide information, those who are responsible may merely engage in "data dumps." Thus, substantial databases may be created, but the important or most important data might not be interpreted and used for policy decisions. Statutes and professional protocols may not recognize the need for clarity of presentation and feedback. Data collection may not include a sense of how data are to be communicated. Even when data have been collected by industry or governmental agencies, institutional barriers may prevent access.

Professionals are likely to experience a tangle of organizations, frustration in acquiring information, and data dumps that load large amounts of information in ways that make it difficult to access and manage (see Heath et al., 2009; Heath and O'Hair, 2009). Further, professionals are unsure that the data and information they obtain are the format and type they are seeking. They question the accuracy and value of the information offered and wonder about its accuracy and relevance. Even when information is obtained, people run into barriers as they seek to exert changes they hope will mitigate the risks they believe they have discovered (O'Hair et al., 2005). A related barrier is the failure on the part of governmental agencies (see Posner, 2002) to agree on the interpretation of information—clearly different disciplines use different nomenclatures to explain their systems and means of adhering to, and making, policy.

Collaboration occurs when a group of autonomous actors engage in an interactive process, using shared rules, norms, and structures, to act or decide on issues that result in mutual benefit and reciprocity (Abramson and Rosenthal, 1995; Wood and Gray, 1991). Following O'Hair et al. (2010), a better understanding is needed of how the actors involved in threat management recognize and leverage each other, not as independent

TABLE 2-1 Online Communication Metric

Metric	Description, Purpose, and/or Objective	Marker	Outcome	Relevance to Other Metrics or Overall Analysis
Semantic Network Analysis	Network mapping of structure or content of threaded messages to describe patterns of interaction.	Use of network mapping software to reduce large datasets of message interactions. Two- and three-dimensional network maps.	Provides patterns (and tendencies) of messages reflecting behavioral regularities, intent, motives, etc.	Easily combined with other markers for charting in situ and longitudinal impressions of message behavior.
Interactive Behaviors—Hostile	Behavioral indices reflecting state of mind (and emotions) and style of communication.	• Flaming • Trolling • Spamming • Cyber-violence	Could be used as either strategic or responsive means of elicitation or retribution. Could track over time.	Any number of metrics could be combined with this.
Credibility of Source	Determines the extent to which source is considered believable by website users.	• Character • Competence • Sociability • Extraversion • Composure • Prestige • Familiarity (Rating scales by coders)	Used to gauge message attractiveness of sources.	Could be used as a component in a clustering of metrics.

		Also develop markers of interaction indicating acceptance and engagement by receivers.		
Collective Voice	A concept that reflects a perception of community or groupness. Collective versus individualist orientation toward interactants.	Language indices such as "we," "our," "us," "them," and "their." Contrast with individualistic orientation—"I," "me," "you," "my."	Initial tracking provides a benchmark of collective orientation. Tracking over time indicates acculturation of user.	Easily triangulated with other metrics to determine assimilation or acculturation.
Chronological Presence of Mind	Linguistic variable reflecting intent, motivation, community orientation, etc.	Verb tense (past, present, future). Can be coded more specifically with perfect, progressive, and emphatic tenses.	Gives an indication of temporal perspective of the communicator.	Easily triangulated with other metrics of assimilation.
Message Framing	Framing is the manner in which communication influences an individual's cognition by selectively emphasizing particular portions of reality while disregarding or downplaying other parts.	• Slant • Structure • Emphasis • Selection • Word choice • Context	Provides an indication of the strategy or approach used by successful or unsuccessful recruiters.	Easily triangulated with other metrics of assimilation.

units but as sources for potential collaboration. One relevant collaboration process is boundary spanning, which allows members to interact with outside stakeholders and enables them to effectively deal with ambiguities of external threats (Golden and Veiga, 2005).

Boundary spanning is viewed as the coordination of experiences, values, context information, expert insight, and the actions of two or more independent organizations. Through boundary spanning, meaningful knowledge is constructed within interorganizational groups, and knowledge is shared freely through collaborative processes such as conversation and joint work (Brown and Duguid, 1991; O'Hair et al., 2010; Orr, 1990; Wenger, 1998). The fields of information science and management studies offer a plentiful stream of studies related to boundary spanning, with many having a focus on knowledge management (Kogut and Zander, 1992; Larsson et al., 1998; Rosenkopf and Nerkar, 2001).

Boundary spanning includes working together with organizations, coordinating activities, and mobilizing resources in the community. Knowledge networks often have the responsibility to formally or informally establish and maintain communication patterns across organizations (Alexander, 1995). At this level, boundary-spanning information systems integrate information flow and coordinate work across "islands" of knowledge (Lamb and Davidson, 2000; Markus et al., 2002). The creation of shared knowledge is feasible when organizations share and improvise local practices through membership in the same work group (Gasson, 2005). By belonging to a community of organizations, mutual engagement in joint enterprise utilizes a shared repertoire of resources (Wenger, 1998). Not only do individual participants belong to multiple communities of practice, "their multiple memberships provide a mediating mechanism that permits the spanning of boundaries between these communities" (Wenger, 1998, p. 123). Future studies should investigate how dimensions of interorganizational collaboration can positively affect data exchange and threat management among organizations in the intelligence and law enforcement communities.

Although this paper provides several areas of inquiry, several other factors have not been fully developed. The very nature of communication actions, the medium through which they are transmitted, and the ultimate intentions form a unique intersection for each individual. At first glance, this might seem like a daunting and overwhelming task. However, communication and behavior are inextricably linked, and the better this connection can be understood, the more likely it is that future predictions about behavior can be made. Moreover, current communication-based theory and methods should be used to both assess the relationship between communication and threatening behavior and develop communication strategies aimed at shifting values, attitudes, beliefs, and behaviors. Thus, communication research could be used to develop messages aimed at reducing threatening communications and behaviors.

It is hoped that, by identifying these areas of communication research, focused inquiry can be generated. More questions were generated than answered in this literature review, and many thorny issues are unlikely to be resolved without a substantial expenditure of resources. The goal of shedding light on the relationship between communication and actual behavior will mostly be accomplished through a triangulation of observational, actuarial, experimental, and case study research. The propositions offered at the outset of this paper suggest that communication theory and practice are intrinsic to the study of threatening behaviors and that finding strategies for managing violent behavior against others will be served by addressing even the most demanding research conundrums.

REFERENCES

Abramson, J.S., and B.B. Rosenthal. 1995. Interdisciplinary and interorganizational collaboration. In R.L. Edwards, ed., *The Encyclopedia of Social Work*, 19th ed., vol. 2 (pp. 1479-1489). Washington, DC: NASW Press.

Alexander, E.R. 1995. *How Organizations Act Together: Interorganizational Coordination in Theory and Practice*. Milwaukee, WI: Gordon and Breach Publishers.

Allen, M., A. Angie, J. Davis, S. Connelly, M. Mumford, and H.D. O'Hair. 2009. Virtual risk: The role of new media in violent and nonviolent ideological groups. In R. Heath and H.D. O'Hair, eds., *Handbook of Risk and Crisis Communication* (pp. 446-470). New York: Routledge.

Avtgis, T.A., and A.S. Rancer. 2008. The relationship between trait verbal aggressiveness and teacher burnout syndrome in K–12 teachers. *Communication Research Reports*, 25:86-89.

Beatty, M.J., and J.C. McCroskey. 1997. It's in our nature: Verbal aggressiveness as temperamental expression. *Communication Quarterly*, 45:446-460.

Biesterfeld, J., and J.R. Meloy. 2008. The public figure assassin as terrorist. In J.R. Meloy, L. Sheridan, and J. Hoffman, eds., *Stalking, Threatening, and Attacking Public Figures* (pp. 143-162). New York: Oxford University Press.

Blazak, R. 2001. White boys to terrorist men: Target recruitment of Nazi skinheads. *American Behavioral Scientist*, 44(6):982-1000.

Bond, C.F., Jr., and B.M. DePaulo. 2006. Accuracy of deception judgments. *Personality and Social Psychology Review*, 10(3):214-234.

Boster, F.J., T.A. Levine, and D. Kazoleas. 1993. The impact of argumentativeness and verbal aggressiveness on strategic diversity and persistence in compliance-gaining behavior. *Communication Quarterly*, 41:405-414.

Brown, J.S., and P. Duguid. 1991. Organizational learning and communities-of-practice: Toward a unified view of working, learning, and innovation. *Organization Science*, 2:40-57.

Burgoon, J.K., and T. Qin. 2006. The dynamic nature of deceptive verbal communication. *Journal of Language and Social Psychology*, 26(1):76-96.

Burgoon, J.K., and V.V. Varadan. 2006. *Workshop on Report on Detecting and Countering IEDs and Related Threats*. Reston, VA: National Science Foundation.

Burgoon, J.K., M. Adkins, J. Kruse, M.L. Jensen, T.O. Meservy, D.P. Twitchell, A. Deokar, J.F. Nunamaker Jr., S. Lu, G. Tsechpenakis, D. Metaxas, and R.E. Younger. 2005. An approach for intent identification by building on deception detection. *Proceedings of the 38th Annual Hawaii International Conference on System Sciences*. Big Island, HI.

Burgoon, J.K., H.D. O'Hair, M. Jensen, and C.H. Miller. 2008. *Information Verification and Assurance Analysis System (IVAAS)*. Technical Report and Proposal to the Defense University Research Instrumentation Program. Norman: University of Oklahoma.

Buunk, B.P. 1991. Jealousy in close relationships: An exchange-theoretical perspective. In P. Salovey, ed., *The Psychology of Jealousy and Envy* (pp. 148-177). New York: Guilford.

Cahn, D.D. 1992. *Conflict in Intimate Relationships*. New York: Guilford.

Canary, D.J., B.H. Spitzberg, and B.A. Semic. 1998. The experience and expression of anger in interpersonal settings. In P.A. Anderson and L.K. Guerrero, eds., *Handbook of Communication and Emotion: Research, Theory, Applications, and Contexts* (pp. 189-213). San Diego, CA: Academic Press.

Caprara, G.V., and C. Pastorelli. 1989. Toward a reorientation of research on aggression. *European Journal of Personality*, 3:121-138.

Carlson, P.J., and G.B. Davis. 1998. An investigation of media selection among directors and managers: From "self" to "other" orientation. *MIS Quarterly*, September:335-358.

Corman, S.R., and J.S. Schiefelbein. 2006. *Communication and Media Strategy in the Jihadi War of Ideas*. Arizona State University, Consortium for Strategic Communication Report No. 0601. Available: http://www.asu.edu/clas/communication/about/csc/ [accessed April 2007].

Daft, R.L., and R. Lengel. 1984. Information richness: A new approach to managerial behavior and organization design. In B.M. Staw and L.L. Cummings, eds., *Research in Organizational Behavior*, vol. 6 (pp. 193-233). Greenwich, CT: JAI Press.

Daft, R.L., J. Sormunen, and D. Parks. 1988. Chief executive scanning, environmental characteristics, and company performance: An empirical study. *Strategic Management Journal*, 9:123-139.

Daly, E.M., W.J. Lancee, and J. Polivy. 1983. A conical model for the taxonomy of emotional experience. *Journal of Personality and Social Psychology*, 45:443-457.

Damphousse, K.R., and B.L. Smith. 2002. The Internet: A terrorist medium for the 21st century. In H.W. Kushner, ed., *Essential Readings on Political Terrorism: Analyses of Problems and Prospects for the 21st Century*. Lincoln: University of Nebraska Press.

Darwin, C. 1872/1998. *The Expression of the Emotions in Man and Animals*, 3rd ed. London, UK: Harper Collins.

DePaulo, B.M., J.J. Lindsay, B.E. Malone, L. Muhlenbruck, K. Charlton, and H. Cooper. 2003. Cues to deception. *Psychological Bulletin*, 129(1):74-118.

Deturck, M.A. 1987. When communication fails: Physical aggression as a compliance-gaining strategy. *Communication Monographs*, 54:106-112.

Dholakia, R.R., M. Zhao, N. Dholakia, and D.R. Fortin. 2000. *Interactivity and Revisits to Websites: A Theoretical Framework*. Available: http://ritim.cba.uri.edu/wp/ [accessed September 2008].

Donohue, W.A., and A.J. Roberto. 1993. Relational development in hostage negotiation. *Human Communication Research*, 20:175-198.

Donohue, W.A., C. Ramesh, and C. Borchgrevink. 1991a. Crisis bargaining: Tracking relational paradox in hostage negotiation. *International Journal of Conflict Management*, 2:257-274.

Donohue, W.A., C. Ramesh, G. Kaufmann, and R. Smith. 1991b. Crisis bargaining in hostage negotiations. *International Journal of Group Tensions*, 21:133-154.

Easterling, D.V., and H. Leventhal. 1989. Contribution of concrete cognition to emotion: Neutral symptoms as elicitors of worry about cancer. *Journal of Applied Psychology*, 74:787-796.

Ekman, P. 1972. Universals and cultural differences in facial expressions of emotions. In J. Cole, ed., *Nebraska Symposium on Motivation, 1971*, vol. 19 (pp. 207-282). Lincoln: University of Nebraska Press.

Ekman, P. 1978. Facial expression. In A.W. Siegman and S. Feldstein, eds., *Nonverbal Behavior and Communication* (pp. 99-116). Hillsdale, NJ: Lawrence Erlbaum Associates.
Ekman, P. 2001. *Telling Lies*. New York: Norton.
Ekman, P., and R.J. Davidson, eds. 1994. *The Nature of Emotion: Fundamental Questions*. Series in Affective Science. New York: Oxford University Press.
Ekman, P., and W.V. Friesen. 1971. Constants across cultures in the face and emotions. *Journal of Personality and Social Psychology*, 17:124-129.
Ekman, P., and W.V. Friesen. 1975. *Unmasking the Face*. Englewood Cliffs, NJ: Prentice Hall.
Ekman, P., W.V. Friesen, M. O'Sullivan, A. Chan, I. Diacoyanno-Tarlatzis, K. Heider, R. Krause, W.A. LeCompte, T. Pitcairn, P.E. Ricci-Bitti, K. Scherer, M. Tomita, and A. Tzavaras. 1987. Universals and cultural differences in the judgments of facial expressions of emotion. *Journal of Personality and Social Psychology*, 54(4):712-717.
Fein, R.A., and B. Vossekuil. 1998. Preventing attacks on public officials and public figures: A secret service perspective. In J.R. Meloy, ed., *The Psychology of Stalking: Clinical and Forensic Perspectives* (pp. 175-191). San Diego, CA: Academic Press.
Fein, R.A., B. Vossekuil, and G.A. Holden. 1995. *Threat Assessment: An Approach to Prevent Targeted Violence*. Washington, DC: National Institute of Justice.
Frijda, N.H. 1986. *The Emotions*. Cambridge, UK: Cambridge University Press.
Frijda, N.H. 1987. Emotion, cognitive structure, and action tendency. *Cognition and Emotion*, 1:115-143.
Fulk, J., and L. Collins-Jarvis. 2001. Wired meetings: Technological mediation of organizational gatherings. In F.M. Jablin and L.L. Putnam, eds., *The New Handbook of Organizational Communication: Advances in Theory, Research, and Methods* (pp. 624-663). Thousand Oaks, CA: Sage.
Gasson, S. 2005. The dynamics of sense making, knowledge, and expertise in collaborative, boundary-spanning design. *Journal of Computer-Mediated Communication*, 10(4):1-26.
Golden, T.D., and J.F. Veiga. 2005. Spanning boundaries and borders: Toward understanding the cultural dimensions of team boundary spanning. *Journal of Managerial Issues*, 17:178-197.
Goldstein, D., and A. Rosenbaum. 1985. An evaluation of the self-esteem of maritally violent men. *Family Relations*, 34:425-428.
Gottman, J.M. 1994. *What Predicts Divorce? The Relationship Between Marital Processes and Marital Outcomes*. Hillsdale, NJ: Lawrence Erlbaum Associates.
Greenberg, B.S. 1976. The effects of language intensity modification on perceived verbal aggressiveness. *Communication Monographs*, 43:130-139.
Guerrero, L.K., and P.A. Andersen. 1998. The dark side of jealousy and envy: Desire, delusion, desperation, and destructive communication. In B.H. Spitzberg and W.R. Cupach, eds., *The Dark Side of Close Relationships* (pp. 33-70). Mahwah, NJ: Lawrence Erlbaum Associates.
Guerrero, L.K., and A.G. La Valley. 2006. Conflict, emotion, and communication. In J.G. Oetzel and S. Ting-Toomey, eds., *The Sage Handbook of Conflict Communication: Integrating Theory, Research, and Practice* (pp. 69-96). Thousand Oaks, CA: Sage.
Guerrero, L.K., M.L. Trost, and S.M. Yoshimura. 2005. Sexual and emotional jealousy. In J. Harvey, A. Wenzel, and S. Sprecher, eds., *The Handbook of Sexuality in Close Relationships* (pp. 311-345). Thousand Oaks, CA: Sage.
Hadden, S.G. 1989. The future of expert systems in government. *Journal of Policy Analysis and Management*, 8:203-208.
Hale, J.L., and J.P. Dillard. 1995. Fear appeals in health promotion campaigns: Too much, too little, or just right? In E. Maibach and R.L. Parrott, eds., *Designing Health Messages: Approaches from Communication Theory and Public Health Practice* (pp. 65-80). Thousand Oaks, CA: Sage.

Hammer, M.R. 2001. Conflict negotiation under crisis conditions. In W.F. Eadie and P.E. Nelson, eds., *The Language of Conflict Resolution* (pp. 57-80). Thousand Oaks, CA: Sage.

Hammer, M.R., and R.G. Rogan. 1997. Negotation models in crisis situations: The value of a communication-based approach. In R.G. Rogan, M.R. Hammer, and C.R. Van Zandt, eds., *Dynamic Processes of Crisis Negotiations: Theory, Research, and Practice* (pp. 9-23). Westport, CT: Praeger.

Hartwig, M., P.A. Granhag, L.A. Strömwall, and A. Vrij. 2005. Detecting deception via strategic disclosure of evidence. *Law and Human Behavior*, 29(4):469-484.

Hartwig, M., P.A. Granhag, L.A. Strömwall, and O. Kronkvist. 2006. Strategic use of evidence during police interviews: When training to detect deception works. *Law and Human Behavior*, 30(5):603-619.

Havill, A. 2001. *The Spy Who Stayed Out in the Cold: The Secret Life of FBI Double Agent Robert Hanssen*. New York: St. Martin's Press.

Heath, R.L., and H.D. O'Hair. 2009. The significance of risk and crisis communication. In R.L. Heath and H.D. O'Hair, eds., *Handbook of Risk and Crisis Communication* (pp. 5-30). New York: Routledge.

Heath, R.L., M. Palenchar, and H.D. O'Hair. 2009. Community building through risk communication infrastructures. In R.L. Heath and H.D. O'Hair, eds., *Handbook of Risk and Crisis Communication* (pp. 471-487). New York: Routledge.

Heider, F. 1958. *The Psychology of Interpersonal Relations*. New York: Wiley.

Heisel, A.D., B.H. La France, and M.J. Beatty. 2003. Self-reported extraversion, neuroticism, and psychoticism as predictors of peer-related verbal aggressiveness and affinity-seeking competence. *Communication Monographs*, 70:1-15.

Hocker, J.L., and W.W. Wilmot. 1998. *Interpersonal Conflict*, 5th ed. Madison, WI: Brown and Benchmark.

Infante, D.A. 1985. Inducing women to be more argumentative: Source credibility effects. *Journal of Applied Communication Research*, 13:33-44.

Infante, D.A. 1987. Aggressiveness. In J.C. McCroskey and J.A. Daly, eds., *Personality and Interpersonal Communication* (pp. 157-192). Newbury Park, CA: Sage.

Infante, D.A., and A.S. Rancer. 1982. A conceptualization and measure of argumentativeness. *Journal of Personality Assessment*, 46:72-80.

Infante, D.A., and A.S. Rancer. 1996. Argumentativeness and verbal aggressiveness: A review of recent theory and research. *Communication Yearbook*, 19:319-351.

Infante, D.A., and C.J. Wigley III. 1986. Verbal aggressiveness: An interpersonal model and measure. *Communication Monographs*, 53:61-69.

Infante, D.A., T.A. Chandler, and J.E. Rudd. 1989. Test of an argumentative skill deficiency model of interspousal violence. *Communication Monographs*, 56:163-177.

Infante, D.A., T.C. Sabourin, J.E. Rudd, and E.A. Shannon. 1990. Verbal aggression in violent and nonviolent marital disputes. *Communication Quarterly*, 38:361-371.

Infante, D.A., B.L. Riddle, C.L. Horvath, and S.A. Tumlin. 1992. Verbal aggressiveness: Messages and reasons. *Communication Quarterly*, 40:116-126.

Izard, C.E. 1990. Facial expressions and the regulation of emotions. *Journal of Personality and Social Psychology*, 58:87-98.

Jensen, J.F. 1998. Interactivity: Tracking a new concept in media and communication studies. *Nordicom Review*, 19:185-204. Available: http://www.nordicom.gu.se/common/publ_pdf/38_jensen.pdf [accessed September 2010].

Jones, T.S. 2000. Emotional communication in conflict: Essence and impact. In W. Eadie and P. Nelson, eds., *The Language of Conflict and Resolution* (pp. 81-104). Thousand Oaks, CA: Sage.

Karayanni, D.A., and G.A. Baltas. 2003. Web site characteristics and business performance: Some evidence from international and business-to-business organizations. *Marketing Intelligence and Planning*, 21:105-114.

Katz, J.E., and R.E. Rice. 2002. The telephone as a medium of faith, hope, terror, and redemption: America, September 11. *Prometheus*, 20(3):247-253.

Kearney, P., T.G. Plax, E.R. Hays, and M.J. Ivey. 1991. College teacher misbehaviors: What students don't like about what teachers say and do. *Communication Quarterly*, 39:309-324.

Kinney, T.A. 1994. An inductively derived typology of verbal aggression and its association to distress. *Human Communication Research*, 21:183-222.

Kogut, B., and U. Zander. 1992. Knowledge of the firm, combinative capabilities, and the replication of technology. *Organization Science*, 9:285-305.

Kotowski, M.R., T.R. Levine, C.R. Baker, and J.M. Bolt. 2009. A multitrait multimethod validity assessment of the verbal aggressiveness and argumentativeness scales. *Communication Monographs*, 76(4):443-462.

Kraut, R., J. Galegher, R. Fish, and B. Chalfonte. 1992. Task requirements and media choice in collaborative writing. *Human-Computer Interaction*, 74:375-407.

Lamb, R., and E. Davidson. 2000. The new computing archipelago: Intranet islands of practice. *International Federation of Information Processing 8.2 Conference Proceedings*, June.

Langdridge, D., and T. Butt. 2004. The fundamental attribution error: A phenomenological critique. *British Journal of Social Psychology*, 43(3):357-369.

Larsson, R., L. Bengtsson, K. Henriksson, and J. Sparks. 1998. The interorganizational learning dilemma: Collective knowledge development in strategic alliances. *Organizational Science*, 9:285-305.

Lazarus, R.S. 1991. *Emotion and Adaptation*. New York: Oxford University Press.

Lengel, R.H., and R.L. Daft. 1988. The selection of communication media as an executive skill. *The Academy of Management Executive*, 2(3):225-232.

Levine, T.R., M.J. Beatty, S. Limon, M.A. Hamilton, R. Buck, and R.M. Chory-Assad. 2004. The dimensionality of the verbal aggressiveness scale. *Communication Monographs*, 71:245-268.

Lewenstein, B.V. 1992. The meaning of "public understanding of science" in the United States after World War II. *Public Understanding of Science*, 1:45-68.

Lewenstein, B.V., and D. Brosard. 2006. *Assessing Models of Public Understanding in ELSI Outreach Materials*. U.S. Department of Energy Grant DE-FG02-01ER63173. Ithaca, NY: Cornell University.

Lewis, M., and J.M. Havliand-Jones, eds. 2000. *Handbook of Emotions*, 2nd ed. New York: Guilford Press.

Maclaran, P., and M. Catterall. 2002. Researching the social web: Marketing information from virtual communities. *Marketing Intelligence and Planning*, 20(6):319-326.

Markus, M.L., A. Majchrzak, and L. Gasser. 2002. A design theory for systems that support emergent knowledge processes. *Management Information Systems Quarterly*, 26(3):179-212.

Martin, M.M., and C.M. Anderson. 1996. Argumentativeness and verbal aggressiveness. *Journal of Social Behavior and Personality*, 11:547-554.

Matusitz, J., and H.D. O'Hair. 2008. The Internet and terrorist networks. In H.D. O'Hair, R.L. Heath, K. Ayotte, and J. Ledlow, eds., *Terrorism: Communication and Rhetorical Perspective* (pp. 383-407). Cresskill, NJ: Hampton Press.

McPherson, M.B., P. Kearney, and T.G. Plax. 2003. The dark side of instruction: Teacher anger as classroom norm violations. *Journal of Applied Communication Research*, 31:76-90.

Meloy, J.R., L. Sheridan, and J. Hoffman. 2008. Public figure stalking, threats, and attacks: The state of the science. In J.R. Meloy, L. Sheridan, and J. Hoffman, eds., *Stalking, Threatening, and Attacking Public Figures* (pp. 3-34). New York: Oxford University Press.

Meservy, T.O., M.L. Jensen, J. Kruse, J.K. Burgoon, and J.F. Nunamaker. 2005. Automatic extraction of deceptive behavioral cues from video. *Intelligence and Security Informatics: Proceedings of the Third Symposium on Intelligence and Security Informatics ISI 2005*. Atlanta, GA: Springer-Verlag.

Moghaddam, F.M. 2005. The staircase to terrorism: A psychological exploration. *American Psychologist*, 60(2):161-169.
Morris, M., and C. Ogan. 1996. The Internet as mass medium. *Journal of Communication*, 46(1):39-51.
Moss, G.A., R. Gunn, and K. Kubacki. 2007. Successes and failures of the mirroring principle: The case of angling and beauty websites. *International Journal of Consumer Studies*, 31:248-257.
Mumford, M.D., K.E. Bedell-Avers, S.T. Hunter, J. Espejo, D. Eubanks, and M.S. Connelly. 2008. Violence in ideological and non-ideological groups: A quantitative analysis of qualitative data. *Journal of Applied Social Psychology*, 38(6):1521-1561.
Myers, S.A., and L.E. Bryant. 2008. Emerging adult siblings' use of verbally aggressive messages as hurtful messages. *Communication Quarterly*, 56:268-283.
O'Hair, H.D. 2004. Measuring risk/crisis communication: Taking strategic assessment and program evaluation to the next level. In *Risk and Crisis Communication: Building Trust and Explaining Complexities When Emergencies Arise* (pp. 5-10).Washington, DC: Consortium of Social Science Associations.
O'Hair, H.D., and M. Cody. 1987. Gender and vocal stress differences during truthful and deceptive information sequences. *Human Relations*, 40:1-14.
O'Hair, H.D., and M.J. Cody. 1994. Deception. In W. Cupack and B. Spitzburg, eds., *The Dark Side of Interpersonal Communication* (pp. 181-214). Hillsdale, NJ: Lawrence Erlbaum Associates.
O'Hair, H.D., R.L. Heath, and J. Becker. 2005. Toward a paradigm of managing communication and terrorism. In H.D. O'Hair, R. Heath, and J. Ledlow, eds., *Community Preparedness, Deterrence, and Response to Terrorism: Communication and Terrorism* (pp. 307-327). Westport, CT: Praeger.
O'Hair, H.D., N. Ploeger, and S. Moore. 2010. Applied communication theory and research. In J. Chesebro, ed., *From 20th Century Beginnings to 21st Century Advances: Developing and Evolving from a Century of Transformation* (pp. 89-106). New York: Oxford University Press.
O'Hair, H.D., K. Kelley, and K. Williams. 2010. Managing community risks through a community-communication infrastructure approach. In H. Canary and R. McPhee, eds., *Communication and Organizational Knowledge: Contemporary Issues for Theory and Practice* (pp. 223-243). New York: Routledge.
Orr, J. 1990. Sharing knowledge, celebrating identity: War stories and community memory in a service culture. In D.S. Middleton and D. Edwards, eds., *Collective Remembering: Memory in Society* (pp. 140-169). Beverley Hills, CA: Sage.
Ortony, A., and T.J. Turner. 1990. What's basic about basic emotions? *Psychology Review*, 97:315-331.
Papacharissi, Z., and A.M. Rubin. 2000. Predictors of Internet use. *Journal of Broadcasting and Electronic Media*, 44(2):175-197.
Pfau, M., and R. Parrot. 1993. *Persuasive Communication Campaigns*. Boston, MA: Allyn and Bacon.
Pigott, T.D., and M.J. Wu. 2008. Methodological issues in meta-analyzing standard deviations: Comment on Bond and DePaulo (2008). *Psychological Bulletin*, 134(4):498-500.
Pines, A., and E. Aronson. 1983. Antecedents, correlates, and consequences of sexual jealousy. *Journal of Personality*, 51:108-136.
Planalp, S. 2003. The unacknowledged role of emotion in theories of close relationships: How do theories feel? *Communication Theory*, 13:78-99.
Pollina, D.A., A.B. Dollins, S.M. Senter, T.E. Brown, I. Pavlidis, J.A. Levine, and A. Ryan. 2006. Facial skin surface temperature changes during a "concealed information" test. *Annals of Biomedical Engineering*, 34(7):1182-1189.

Porter, C.E. 2004. A typology of virtual communities: A multi-disciplinary foundation for future research. *Journal of Computer-Mediated Communication*, 10(1). Available: http://jcmc.indiana.edu/vol10/issue1/porter.html [accessed January 2011].

Posner, P.L. 2002. *Intergovernmental Partnership in a National Strategy to Enhance State and Local Preparedness.* GAO-02-547T. Washington, DC: U.S. General Accounting Office.

Prunty, A.M., D.W. Klopf, and S. Ishii. 1990. Argumentativeness: Japanese and American tendencies to approach and avoid conflict. *Communication Research Reports*, 7:75-79.

Rafaeli, S. 1988. Interactivity: From new media to communication. In R.P. Hawkins and J.M. Wiemann, eds., *Advancing Communication Science: Merging Mass and Interpersonal Processes* (pp. 110-134). Newbury Park, CA: Sage.

Rancer, A.S., and A.M. Nicotera. 2007. Aggressive communication. In B.B. Whaley and W. Samter, eds., *Explaining Communication: Contemporary Theories and Exemplars* (pp. 129-146). Mahwah, NJ: Lawrence Erlbaum Associates.

Reddy, M., R. Borum, J. Berglund, B. Vossekuil, R. Fein, and W. Modzeleski. 2001. Evaluating risk for targeted violence in schools: Comparing risk assessment, threat assessment, and other approaches. *Psychology in the Schools*, 38:157-171.

Renn, O. 2009. Risk communication: Insights and requirements for designing successful communication programs on health and environmental hazards. In R.L. Heath and H.D. O'Hair, eds., *Handbook of Risk and Crisis Communication* (pp. 80-98). New York: Routledge.

Rogan, R.C., and B.H. La France. 2003. An examination of the relationship between verbal aggressiveness, conflict management strategies, and conflict interaction goals. *Communication Quarterly*, 51:458-469.

Rogan, R.G., and M.R. Hammer. 1994. Crisis negotiations: A preliminary investigation of facework in naturalistic conflict. *Journal of Applied Communication Research*, 22:216-231.

Rogan, R.G., and M.R. Hammer. 1995. Assessing message affect in crisis negotiations: An exploratory study. *Human Communication Research*, 21:553-574.

Rogan, R.G., and M.R. Hammer. 2002. Crisis/hostage negotiations: Conceptualizations of a communication-based approach. In H. Giles, ed., *Law Enforcement, Communication, and Community* (pp. 229-254). Amsterdam, The Netherlands: John Benjamins.

Rogan, R.G., and M.R. Hammer. 2006. The emerging field of crisis/hostage negotiation: A communication-based perspective. In J.G. Oetzel and S. Ting-Toomey, eds., *The Sage Handbook of Conflict Communication: Integrating Theory, Research, and Practice* (pp. 451-478). Thousand Oaks, CA: Sage.

Rogan, R.G., and B.H. La France. 2003. An examination of the relationship between verbal aggressiveness, conflict management strategies, and conflict interaction goals. *Communication Quarterly*, 51:458-469.

Rogan, R.G., M.R. Hammer, and C.R. Van Zandt, eds. 1997a. *Dynamic Processes of Crisis Negotiations: Theory, Research, and Practice.* Westport, CT: Praeger.

Rogan, R.G., M.R. Hammer, and C.R. Van Zandt. 1997b. Dynamic processes of crisis negotiations: An overview. In R.G. Rogan, M.R. Hammer, and C.R. Van Zandt, eds., *Dynamic Processes of Crisis Negotiations: Theory, Research, and Practice* (pp. 1-8). Westport, CT: Praeger.

Roloff, M.E., and J.M. Jordan. 1992. Achieving negotiation goals: The "fruits and foibles" of planning ahead. In L.L. Putnam and M.E. Roloff, eds., *Communication and Negotiation* (pp. 21-45). Newbury Park, CA: Sage.

Rosenkopf, L., and A. Nerkar. 2001. Beyond local search: Boundary-spanning, exploration and impact in the optical disc industry. *Strategic Management Journal*, 22:287-306.

Rubin, A.M. 1993. Audience activity and media use. *Communication Monographs*, 60:98-103.

Rubin, A.M. 1994. Media uses and effects: A uses-and-gratifications perspective. In J. Bryant and D. Zillmann, eds., *Media Effects: Advances in Theory and Research* (pp. 417-436). Hillsdale, NJ: Lawrence Erlbaum Associates.

Ruiter, R.A.C., C. Abraham, and G. Kok. 2001. Scary warnings and rational precautions: A review of the psychology of fear appeals. *Psychology and Health*, 16:613-630.

Sabourin, T.C., D.A. Infante, and J.E. Rudd. 1993. Verbal aggression in marriages: A comparison of violent, distressed but nonviolent, and nondistressed couples. *Human Communication Research*, 20:245-267.

Scherer, K.R., and H.G. Wallbott. 1994. Evidence for university and cultural variation of differential emotion response patterning. *Journal of Personality and Social Psychology*, 66:310-328.

Sebastian, R.J., R.D. Parke, L. Berkowitz, and S.G. West. 1978. Film violence and verbal aggression: A naturalistic study. *Journal of Communication* 28(3):164-171.

Sereno, K.K., M. Welch, and D. Braaten. 1987. Interpersonal conflict: Effects of variations in manner of expressing anger and justification for anger upon perceptions of appropriateness, competence, and satisfaction. *Journal of Applied Communication Research*, 15:128-143.

Shaver, P.R., J. Schwartz, D. Kirson, and C. O'Connor. 1987. Emotion knowledge: Further explorations of a prototype approach. *Journal of Personality and Social Psychology*, 52:1061-1086.

Sillars, A.L. 1980. Attributions and communication in roommate conflicts. *Communication Monographs*, 47:180-200.

Sillars, A., L.J. Roberts, K.E. Leonard, and T. Dun. 2000. Cognition during marital conflict: The relationship of thought and talk. *Journal of Social and Personal Relationships*, 17:479-502.

Simonelli, C.J., and K.M. Ingram. 1998. Psychological distress among men experiencing physical and emotional abuse in heterosexual dating relationships. *Journal of Interpersonal Violence*, 13:667-681.

Smith, S.S. 2008a. From violent words to violent deed: Assessing risk from FBI threatening communication cases. In J.R. Meloy, L. Sheridan, and J. Hoffman, eds., *Stalking, Threatening, and Attacking Public Figures* (pp. 435-455). New York: Oxford University Press.

Smith, S.S. 2008b. From violent words to violent deeds? Assessing risk from threatening communications. Doctoral dissertation abstract. *International Journal of Speech, Language and the Law*, 15:105-107.

Snyder, G.H., and P. Diesing. 1977. *Conflict Among Nations*. Princeton, NJ: Princeton University Press.

Sohn, D., and B. Lee. 2005. Dimensions of interactivity: Differential effects of social and psychological factors. *Journal of Computer-Mediated Communication*, 10(3). Available: http://jcmc.indiana.edu/vol10/issue3/sohn.html [accessed September 2010].

Song, J.H., and G.M. Zinkhan. 2008. Determinants of perceived web site interactivity. *Journal of Marketing*, 72:99-113.

Stanton, J.J. 2002. Terrorism in cyberspace: Terrorists will exploit and widen the gap between governing structures and the public. *American Behavioral Scientist*, 45(6):1017-1032.

Stephenson, M.T., and K. Witte. 2001. Creating fear in a risky world: Generating effective health risk messages. In R.E. Rice and C.K. Atkins, eds., *Public Communication Campaigns*, 3rd ed. (pp. 88-102). Thousand Oaks, CA: Sage.

Steuer, J. 1992. Defining virtual reality: Dimensions determining telepresence. *Journal of Communication*, 42:73-93.

Suzuki, S., and A.S. Rancer. 1994. Argumentativeness and verbal aggressiveness: Testing for conceptual and measurement equivalence across cultures. *Communication Monographs*, 61:256-278.

Trevino, L.K., J. Webster, and E.W. Stein. 2000. Making connections: Complementary influences on communication media choices, attitudes, and use. *Organization Science*, 11(2):163-182.

Ting-Toomey, S., and A. Kurogi. 1998. Facework competence in intercultural conflict: An updated face-negotiation theory. *International Journal of Intercultural Relations*, 22:187-225.

Vangelisti, A.L. 1994. Messages that hurt. In W.R. Cupach and B.H. Spitzberg, eds., *The Dark Side of Interpersonal Communication* (pp. 53-82). Hillsdale, NJ: Lawrence Erlbaum Associates.

Vangelisti, A.L., and L.P. Crumley. 1998. Reactions to messages that hurt: The influence of relational contexts. *Communication Monographs*, 65:173-196.

Vangelisti, A.L., and R.J. Sprague. 1998. Guilt and hurt: Similarities, distinctions, and conversational strategies. In P.A. Andersen and L.L. Guerrero, eds., *Handbook of Communication and Emotion: Research, Theory, Applications, and Contexts* (pp. 123-154). San Diego, CA: Academic Press.

Vrij, A. 2000. *Detecting Lies and Deceit: The Psychology of Lying and Implications for Professional Practice*. Chichester, UK: John Wiley and Sons.

Weick, K.E. 1979. *The Social Psychology of Organizing*. Reading, MA: Addison-Wesley.

Wenger, E. 1998. *Communities of Practice: Learning, Meaning, and Identity*. New York: Cambridge University Press.

White, G.L., and P.E. Mullen. 1989. *Jealousy: Theory, Research, and Clinical Strategies*. New York: Guilford.

Willard, N.E. 2007. *Cyberbullying and Cyberthreats: Responding to the Challenge of Online Social Aggression, Threats, and Distress*. Champaign, IL: Research Press.

Witte, K. 1992a. Putting the fear back into fear appeals: The extended parallel process model. *Communication Monographs*, 59:329-349.

Witte, K. 1992b. The role of threat and efficacy in AIDS prevention. *International Quarterly of Communication Health Education*, 12:225-249.

Witte, K. 1998. Fear as motivator, fear as inhibitor: Using EPPM to explain fear appeal successes and failures. In P.A. Anderson and L.K. Guerrero, eds., *The Handbook of Communication and Emotion* (pp. 423-450). New York, NY: Academic Press.

Witte, K., and M. Allen. 2000. A meta-analysis of fear appeals: Implications for effective public health campaigns. *Health Education and Behavior*, 27(5):591-615.

Wood, J.T. 2000. *Relational communication: Continuity and Change in Personal Relationships* 2nd ed. Belmont, CA: Wadsworth.

Wood, D.J., and B. Gray. 1991. Toward a comprehensive theory of collaboration. *Journal of Applied Behavioral Science*, 27:139-167.

Wynne, B. 1995. Public understanding of science. In S. Jasanoff, G.E. Markle, J.C. Petersen, and T. Pinch, eds., *Handbook of Science and Technology Studies* (pp. 361-388). Thousand Oaks, CA: Sage.

Ziman, J. 1992. Not knowing, needing to know, and wanting to know. In B.V. Lewenstein, ed., *When Science Meets the Public* (pp. 13-20). Washington, DC: American Association for the Advancement of Science.

Zmud, R., M. Lind, and F. Young. 1990. An attribute space for organizational communication channels. *Information Systems Research*, 1(4):440-457.

Zuckerman, M., and R.E. Driver. 1985. Telling lies: Verbal and nonverbal correlates of deception. In A.W. Siegman and S. Feldstein, eds., *Multichannel Integrations of Nonverbal Behavior* (pp. 129-147). Hillsdale, NJ: Lawrence Erlbaum Associates.

Approaching and Attacking Public Figures: A Contemporary Analysis of Communications and Behavior

J. Reid Meloy

There has been significant research during the past decade on abnormal or threatening communication and its relationship to escalation, approach, or attack behavior toward public figures (Meloy et al., 2008b). This paper is a review and critical integration of that research, which is pertinent to the operational needs of both public and private security, law enforcement, and intelligence agencies tasked with protecting public figures. Included are findings from new empirical studies (James et al., 2009b, 2010a, 2010b; Meloy et al., 2010; Unsgaard and Meloy, 2011) and theoretical advances not yet empirically tested.

The paper is divided into two sections: problematic approaches and attacks. The former refers to any behavior that entails physical movement toward a target that is potentially disruptive or threatening. The latter refers to any near-lethal approach, attack, or assassination of a targeted individual. This division is not arbitrary. It is necessary given the disparate research that has been conducted on samples of problematic approachers and samples of attackers and, in some cases, the divergence of results. It is the author's hope that detailing these differences and similarities will broaden and deepen the understanding of such behaviors and also contribute to advances in operational research while ensuring the safety of public figures.

PROBLEMATIC APPROACHES

Predicting Movement from Communication to Approach

A detailed analysis of six studies, five of which were random samples, of problematic approaches to public figures, both politicians and celebrities, in the United States and Europe indicates a high degree of consistency across six headings that predict movement from communication to an approach (Meloy et al., 2010). The six studies in this analysis (Dietz et al., 1991a, 1991b; Scalora et al., 2002a, 2002b; James et al., 2009a; Meloy et al., 2008a) utilized variables that were similar enough to each other to warrant these six headings. They also provided quantitative data that show a statistically significant difference between approachers and nonapproachers toward the six samples of public figures. The following headings indicate the direction of a *greater likelihood* of an approach:

- No threatening communications
- Serious mental illness
- Requests for help
- Multiple means of communication
- Multiple contacts and targets
- No antagonistic communications

No threatening communications refers to the absence of an expressed desire to do harm to, or have physical harm occur to, a target. *Serious mental illness* refers to the presence of psychosis, indicated by evidence of hallucinations, delusions, or formal thought disorder, during the activity of concern. *Requests for help* refers to the subject asking for help from the target. *Multiple means of communication* refers to the subject using at least two methods of communication, such as writing letters, telephoning, e-mailing, sending gifts or enclosures, or faxing. *Multiple contacts or targets* is the most disparate heading and combines a subject's repetitive contact of a target through any means of communication and the subject's contact of other public figure targets—both have the characteristics of repetitiveness and dispersion. *No antagonistic communications* refers to the absence of any hostile, abusive, or degrading aspects to the communications.

Four of these six studies also conducted logistic regressions to see how accurately an approach could be predicted. Overall correct classification ranged from 76 to 83 percent, which is 25 to 30 percent better than chance, depending on the base rates for approach in each study. Although the predictor variables across the four studies differed, *multiple communications and/or contacts with other targets* emerged as a predictor variable in all four studies. It appears that a common thread across these predictor studies, as well as the other two studies, is a level of energy and fixation on the part of the subject as a necessary prelude to approaching the target, operationally measured by multiple communications to the target and/or contacts with other public figures.

Although the consistency of these findings is promising, further research is necessary to cross-validate the results. Research designs could simply compare random samples of both approachers and nonapproachers to learn whether these six variables continued to both discriminate between the two groups and function in some circumstances as predictors of a problematic approach.

The operational application of these findings, heretofore individually known but not integrated prior to this study (Meloy et al., 2010), was somewhat misguided. A proportion of subjects whose communication characteristics are the *opposite* of these variables will move from communication to approach. This statistical reality was often overlooked in interpretations of the early research by readers who focused on significant differences between approachers and nonapproachers instead of actual frequencies. The assumption made by readers of this research was that significantly less difference meant that the lesser category had a zero frequency of the behavior. This is a logical error but appears to have become operationalized in some threat assessments—for example, the false belief that if there is no communicated threat, there is no risk, or that those who make a direct threat do not pose a threat. Consider the following data, which indicate the proportion of subjects who directly threatened a public figure and then *did make* a subsequent approach:

- 23 percent (Dietz et al., 1991a)
- 33 percent (Dietz et al., 1991b)
- 21 percent (Scalora et al., 2002a)
- 41 percent (Scalora et al., 2002b)
- 35 percent (Meloy et al., 2008a)

Even though these percentages are, in most cases, significantly lower than those for subjects who directly threatened but did not subsequently approach, they tended to be minimized, and often dismissed, when the results of the studies (particularly the Dietz studies) were informally discussed by threat assessment professionals. The within-study interpretations of these data were also problematic. For example, concerning threats and approaches to members of Congress, Dietz et al. (1991b) wrote, "Subjects who sent threats to a member of Congress were significantly less likely to pursue a face-to-face encounter with him or her" (p. 1466). This is statistically accurate but could be incorrectly interpreted as meaning that articulation of a direct threat *would reduce risk* in any one subject who threatened—an interpretation that did not apply to one-third of their sample.

Future studies should emphasize this point and detail not only significant differences but also frequencies, effect size of the differences (preferably measured in odds ratios), and confidence intervals of the odds ratios. Also, Receiver Operating Characteristic analysis can be used to interpret predictive findings to ensure that base rates do not influence predictive outcome statements. The difficult problem of applying nomothetic (large-group) data to an individual case, wherein membership in a class does not necessarily imply individual predictive accuracy, also should be noted (Hart et al., 2007).

Behavioral Pathway, Motivation, and Mental Disorder

Odd, inappropriate, bizarre, or threatening communication addressed to a public figure cannot be fully understood by itself without other information about the sender, especially the behavioral pathway, motivation, and nature of the sender's mental disorder. *Behavioral pathway* refers to the path along which an individual might progress in moving from communicating with a target to close physical proximity to the target. It was first mentioned by Dietz and Martell (1989) and then systematically studied by Fein and colleagues (1995) and Fein and Vossekuil (1998, 1999); later it was demarcated into stages by Calhoun and Weston (2003). Most recently it has been applied to studies of problematic approaches by various individuals to the British Royal Family.

James et al. (2009a) divided the stages into preapproach communications, communications and approach, approach without communications, unsuccessful breach of security, successful breach of security, and attack. Such a pathway analysis yields important behavioral findings, most notably the degree to which a perpetrator is influenced by both motivation and mental disorder. *Motivation* refers to the reason for the behavioral approach; it can be driven by "psychotic action" (Junginger, 1996)—behaviors driven by delusions or hallucinations. The nature of the mental disorder, if present, is most important when analyzed according to symptoms and behaviors—not diagnosis—and whether or not it causes, mediates, correlates with, or is unrelated to the motivation for the approach.

Three recent typologies attempt to address these aspects of public figure stalkers. Phillips (2006, 2008) identified five categories among an unknown number of subjects who approached, in a problematic way, protectees of the U.S. Secret Service: resentful, pathologically obsessed, infamy seeking, intimacy seeking, and nuisance or attention seeking. His typology focused on motive, positive symptoms of psychosis, and intent to do harm but did not incorporate a behavioral pathway analysis. James et al. (2009a) identified eight motivational types among a random sample of 275 problematic approachers toward the British Royal Family: (1) delusions of royal identity, (2) amity seekers, (3) intimacy seekers, (4) sanctuary and help seekers, (5) royally persecuted, (6) counselors, (7) querulants (vexatious litigants), and (8) chaotics (those whose behaviors and motivations were highly disorganized). Their motivational typology was studied in relation to both the behavioral pathway and serious mental disorder.

In *The Stalking Risk Profile*, MacKenzie et al. (2009) identified eight motivational categories for stalkers of public figures: (1) resentful, (2) intimacy seekers, (3) incompetent suitors, (4) predatory (sexual motivation), (5) help seekers, (6) attention seekers, (7) the chaotic, and (8) unclassified. The *profile* was designed for risk management of such cases and is a structured professional judgment instrument (Monahan, 2000). Although typologies may seem irrelevant to operational tasks, they are not. A typology developed from a random sample of subjects of concern can bring more efficiency to the assignment and utilization of protective intelligence resources. Such work, along with research on mental disorders and behavioral pathways, could eventuate in an iterative decision-tree model for estimating the risk of problematic approaches toward or stalking of a protectee, much like the Classification of Violence Risk, developed to help predict the risk of short-term violence among persons discharged from acute care psychiatric facilities (Monahan et al., 2001; Monahan, 2010).

To determine operational validity, typologies need to be empirically tested for both inter-rater reliability and various kinds of validity across a number of variables important to protection, such as the prediction of a successful breach of security. The Phillips' (2006, 2008) typology has not yet been empirically tested, but holds promise given its derivation from actual threateners and approachers identified by the U.S. Secret Service. Moreover, across all of the typologies there appears to be a supraordinate variable called *fixation* (from the Latin *figo*, meaning to be bound fast) that has both clinical and behavioral significance.

Fixation

Emerging research indicates the importance of *fixation*, an intense preoccupation with an individual, activity, or idea (Meloy et al., 2008b). Normal fixations are a part of everyday life and include such states as romantic love, parental devotion, intense loyalty, and adulation. Pathological fixations are obsessive preoccupations that typically result in deterioration of the subject's intimate, social, and occupational lives (Leets et al., 1995; Mullen et al., 2009a; Schlesinger, 2006). Such pathological fixations focus on a *person* or *cause*, the latter an intensely personal grievance or quest for justice that inhibits effective social functioning and alienates others. Research in Europe indicates that fixation on a cause is related to risk of attack. In a study of nonterrorist attacks on Western European politicians between 1990 and 2003, 50 percent of attackers were found to be fixated on a cause (James et al., 2007; $N = 24$). In a study of attacks on the British Royal Family between 1778 and 1994 (James et al., 2008; $N = 23$), 63 percent of subjects whose motivation could be discerned ($n = 19$) were fixated on a cause.

Although it is difficult to make this distinction in the U.S. Secret Service Exceptional Case Study Project (ECSP) (Fein and Vossekuil, 1999), 67 percent of near-lethal approachers, attackers, and assassins had a grievance, as well as motivations that suggested focus on a cause, such as avenging a perceived wrong, bringing national attention to a perceived problem, saving the country/world, and bringing about political change (Fein and Vossekuil, 1998, 1999). Fixation on a cause may be a moderating variable between problematic approach and intent to attack, but it has not been empirically studied. Such fixations are distinguished from political extremism, which usually emerges in interactions of an actual or virtual group on the fringes of the traditional political process and is not as intensely personalized.

The nature of the fixations evident in abnormal communications to public figures has been studied in the context of British and Western European attackers (James et al., 2007, 2008). Although they may predict certain subsequent behavioral pathways or escalations, the empirical question is whether fixation on a cause incrementally contributes to risk of an attack on a public figure, especially politicians and government officials. The supraordinate, and perhaps clinically obscure concept of fixation, moreover, is often evident in warning behaviors.

Warning Behaviors

Emerging research supports the belief that warning behaviors are important and should be construed as much broader than a specific threat (Meloy et al., 2004b; Scalora et al., 2002a, 2002b, 2003). Warning behaviors are dynamic and acute behaviors that precede an act of targeted violence, are related to it, and are therefore a risk factor for it. Warning behaviors show an intense and accelerating effort to further a particular quest, usually some highly personal cause. They often predict an approach (Meloy et al., 2010), but with some exceptions (Scalora et al., 2003). Intensity is usually measured by frequency of contact, duration of contact, multiple means of contact, and multiple contacts with other figures (target dispersion) and is associated in the research with the presence of serious mental disorder (James et al., 2009a; Scalora et al., 2002b).

Warning behaviors are also present in research on attacks. In contemporary Western European attacks (James et al., 2007), 46 percent of subjects evidenced warning behaviors before attacking[1] and were more likely at the time of the attack to have a mental disorder (phi = 0.77 effect size), to be psychotic (0.65), and to show clear evidence of delusional beliefs (0.65). In the ECSP study (Fein and Vossekuil, 1998, 1999)—despite the very low frequency of direct threats toward the target or law enforcement (7 percent)—most subjects had a history of verbal or written communication *about* the target (77 percent); one out of four communicated to the target (23 percent); and 63 percent had a history of indirect, conditional, or direct threats *about* the target.

Specific warning behaviors may be another moderating variable between the research on problematic approaches and attacks. As yet, there are no studies of specific warning behaviors as predictors of a targeted attack. There are many case studies, though, that have retrospectively identified certain warning behaviors after an attack as predictors of that attack, but such circular reasoning does not advance predictive science. It would be most useful to determine both the specificity (accuracy of not predicting) and the sensitivity (accuracy of predicting) of certain warning behaviors in relationship to an attack—a task easier said than done. Moreover, the fundamental difficulty with warning behaviors is a lack of clarity in definition.

Meloy et al. (unpublished) have recently proposed that warning behaviors can be divided into seven categories:

- Pathway warning behavior—acts that indicate research, planning, preparation, or implementation of an attack (Calhoun and Weston, 2003).
- Fixation warning behavior—increasingly pathological preoccupations with a public figure or a highly personalized cause (Mullen et al., 2009a).
- Identification warning behavior—a psychological desire to be a "pseudocommando" (Dietz, 1986; Knoll, 2010); development of a "warrior mentality" (Hempel et al., 1999); interest in and study of previous assassins or public figure attackers; or fascination with weapons, as indicated by collection, approach, skill development, or fantasy-based associations (Meloy, 1992a).

---

[1] In the European study, warning behaviors included posters, newspaper advertisements, attempted lawsuits against the government, chaotic deluded letters to politicians and the police, threatening letters, leafleting the public, telling friends of intent to attack, and in one case attempted self-immolation in front of the eventual victim's workplace. In some cases, these warning behaviors went on for years.

- Novel aggression warning behavior—acts of violence unrelated to the planned and targeted attack that are committed for the first time.
- Energy-burst warning behavior—increase in the frequency, duration, or variety of any warning behavior prior to an attack.
- Leakage warning behavior—communication to a third party of intent to do harm to a target through an attack (O'Toole, 2000; Meloy and O'Toole, in press).
- Direct-threat warning behavior—communication of a direct threat to the target or law enforcement before an attack on a public figure.

These seven categories have face validity and are commonly encountered in threat assessment cases, but they have not been subjected to empirical testing to determine their inter-rater reliability or their validity in predicting an attack.

Grandiosity and Entitled Reciprocity

Grandiosity and entitled reciprocity have emerged as two important psychological characteristics of subjects who approach public figures. They suggest both psychopathology in general and pathological narcissism—a sense of specialness that diminishes empathy for others. Grandiosity, an exaggerated sense of self-importance evident in communications, was tested in a logistic regression model in a study of those who approached or did not approach members of the British Royal Family (James et al., 2010a).

A regression for a model comprising the single factor of grandiosity produced an Area Under the Curve (AUC) of 0.74 (95 percent confidence interval 0.65 to 0.82) and correctly predicted almost 74 percent of the cases—nearly 74 percent of the approachers and over 73 percent of the nonapproachers. The effect size was moderate (phi = 0.47). Dietz and Martell (1989) found in their study more than 20 years ago that those who approached celebrities were significantly more likely ($X^2 = 4.85, p < .03$) to evidence an excessive sense of self-importance or uniqueness (52 percent) than those who did not approach (36 percent). If subjects who problematically approached members of Congress took a "special constituent role," it significantly increased the risk of an approach (46 versus 16 percent, $X^2 = 7.77, p = .0053$). Grandiosity can be somewhat grounded in reality (e.g., "I can dramatically influence the votes in my district!") or delusional (e.g., "I am the president!"). In many cases, grandiosity among such subjects compensates in fantasy for real-life failures in both work and love.

Grandiosity is a facet of pathological narcissism, an aspect of personality that is quite apparent in stalkers (Meloy, 1998; Mullen et al.,

2009b) and is an abnormal variant of narcissism, most clearly defined by Rothstein (1980) as "a felt quality of perfection" (p. 4). Grandiosity is also apparent in the attack research, specifically the ECSP study. Fein and Vossekuil (1998, 1999) reported that in 38 percent of principal incidents of near-lethal approach, attack, or assassination ($N = 74$) there was evidence that attention/notoriety was a goal. Of the eight motives they cited for attacks, grandiosity, or the wish to achieve such importance, can be inferred in five: (1) to achieve notoriety/fame, (2) to bring national attention to a perceived problem, (3) to save the country or the world, (4) to achieve a special relationship with the target, or (5) to bring about political change.

Years after the assassination of President John F. Kennedy in 1963 (Bugliosi, 2007), a close female friend of Lee Harvey Oswald reflected on Oswald's personality in Minsk during the years 1959 to 1962: "I could paint a portrait of him as someone who thinks too much of himself but doesn't work to become the person he wants to be.... The most important thing for Lee was that he wanted to become famous. Idea number one. He was fanatic about it, I think. Goal number one. Show that he was different from others, and you know, he achieved this goal" (Mailer, 1995, p. 321). A psychiatric social worker at the Youth House in Manhattan where Oswald was briefly placed as an adolescent for chronic truancy recorded similar findings: "He acknowledged fantasies about being all-powerful and being able to do anything he wanted. When asked if this ever involved hurting or killing people, he said that it did sometimes but [he] refused to elucidate on it" (Mailer, 1995, p. 365). She later wrote: "There is a rather pleasant, appealing quality about this emotionally starved, affectionless youngster which grows as one speaks to him" (p. 365).

Entitled reciprocity is the belief that a particular public figure owes the subject time and attention because of the time and attention the subject has paid to the public figure (Meloy et al., 2008b). It is also an aspect of pathological narcissism and is related to grandiosity: The subject's importance demands that he receive the attention he deserves. In the British Royal Family study (James et al., 2010a), three motivations together accounted for nearly 72 percent of cases in which the communicators went on to approach—those with delusions of royalty, amity seekers, and intimacy seekers. Among all these motivations is the subject's often delusional belief that he or she is owed a debt of gratitude through blood ties, friendship, or love.

Entitled reciprocity, however, has not been measured but may be an important predictor of resentment and perhaps aggression in certain subjects who are shunned by their public figure target. This could develop over time when communications are not responded to, or it could be an acutely negative emotional reaction when a highly anticipated personal encounter with the public figure results in disappointment or the humiliation of being ignored. An example of grandiosity and entitled reciprocity from a letter writer to Prince Charles appears below (from author's files, courtesy of the Fixated Threat Assessment Centre, London):

> Dear Charles—God dam it. God dam *you*! Charles Prince of Wales! You know that the Catholic Church is a cult, right? You do know that, don't you? Well, it is. And you shouldn't be worshipping the Virgin Mary. She's not the Queen of Heaven. I AM! I'm God's wife, and you better make room for me there now! How dare you make me grovel in the dirt. Charles, I'm your Heavenly Mother! And you best start respecting me as such with a whole lot of hugs and kisses (on the cheek), well wishes, and tender loving care, or you are going to die a very long death starting right now! Stick to the Word of God, Charles.

Electronic Communications to Public Figures

Although it might seem that the written letter to Prince Charles is a relic of the past given the various social media platforms available today for communications, there is virtually no research contrasting the use of electronic communications (e.g., e-mails) toward public figures—with one exception, described by Schoeneman-Morris et al. (2007). This random study of e-mails and letters to members of the U.S. Congress found that letter writers were more problematic in that they were significantly more likely to exhibit symptoms of severe mental illness, engage in multiple target contacts, use multiple methods of contact, and approach. In fact, e-mail senders focused on government concerns, used obscene language, and displayed disorganization significantly more often. Threatening language was found in about half of all communications, with no significant differences between the two types of communication.

The research possibilities concerning electronic communications are endless. Any attempts to contrast samples of written letters and e-mails to public figures, with a focus on variables predicting a problematic approach, would contribute to this nascent area of investigation. Historically, written communications to public figures held a central place in threat assessment investigation, until challenged by the work of Fein and Vossekuil (1998, 1999), and further research could prove operationally useful.

Making or Posing a Threat

The distinction between making and posing a threat, first enunciated by Fein et al. (1995) and utilized in the ECSP study, has permeated the threat assessment community over the past 15 years as an important theoretical construct and operational focus (Calhoun, 1998; Calhoun and Weston, 2003, 2008). Calhoun and Weston have challenged the assumptions that those who make a direct threat pose the greatest risk and that articulated threats are central to threat assessment. The challenge derived from the fact that *none* of the subjects who attacked or assassinated a U.S. public figure in the second half of the twentieth century communicated a direct threat to law enforcement or the target beforehand (Fein and Vossekuil, 1999). Subsequent research with other data on attacks of public figures makes clear that suspicious behavior ("warning behaviors") should be considered more important than a directly communicated threat when assessing the risk of an approach (Meloy et al., 2004b) to any public figure. For instance, James et al. (2007) also found that *none* of the subjects who attacked a Western European politician between 1990 and 2004 had directly communicated a threat beforehand. Such findings have moved threats from principal actor to supporting role in the theater of public figure threat assessment. However, warning behaviors—the somewhat obscure elements of a decision called "posing a threat"—are not clearly enunciated in the research, as noted earlier, and characteristics that lead to the decision that a subject "poses a threat" are also unknown. To further complicate matters, in certain cases, those who make threats also pose threats (Scalora et al., 2002a, 2002b).

To yield predictive data, the elements of such behaviors must be consistently defined and further studied, which could include a standardized definition of "posing a threat" and identifying the decision-making tree that leads to the perception of a "posed threat" by threat assessment professionals. One approach is to empirically study the various levels of concern and threat currently utilized by public and private security agencies to determine if they are reliably applied to various cases and the degree to which they predict certain approach behaviors or necessary interventions to curtail such approaches (e.g., arrest, hospitalization, surveillance). An important group that also merits study consists of those who problematically approach a public figure without communicating beforehand and without intending to attack. This group has been mostly neglected in the research to date. In the British Royal Family study (James et al., 2009a), this group was found to be more likely to behave in an intimidating manner, more likely to attempt to breach security, and much less likely to be fixated on the target than were approachers who communicated beforehand. This group (approach/no communication/no intent to attack) was not utilized as a comparison group in the ECSP research, which might have provided useful information.

ATTACKS AND ASSASSINATIONS

Mental Disorders, Attacks, and Assassinations

Research indicates the importance of mental disorders in a large proportion of subjects who attack public figures (Fein and Vossekuil, 1998, 1999; James et al., 2007, 2008; Meloy et al., 2004b). In the ECSP study, the finding of a substantial presence of mental disorder contrasts with the recommendations that diminished the importance of mental disorder (Fein and Vossekuil, 1999): 61 percent of subjects had been evaluated by a mental health professional, 43 percent had a history of delusions and were delusional during their attack or near-lethal approach, and 21 percent had a history of auditory hallucinations. However, Fein and Vossekuil made two important points: (1) within the delusion, the behavior toward the target may be quite rational and (2) focusing on the "thinking that leads a person to see assassination as an acceptable, or necessary action" (p. 332) is operationally much more useful than labeling or diagnosing the person with a particular mental disorder. Their position is supported by a large meta-analysis of the relationship between psychosis and violence (Douglas et al., 2009), which found that studies coded at the level of the symptom had significantly higher effect sizes, particularly active positive symptoms (delusions, hallucinations, etc.), when studying the relationship between violence and psychosis.

The operational implications of these findings and opinions are significant. Threat assessment professionals will find the description of behaviors and symptoms related to a mental disorder more useful than the particular diagnostic label. For example, discovering through investigative efforts that a particular subject has paranoid schizophrenia is much less relevant to threat assessment than noting that the subject believes the public target is an alien from another planet and needs to be killed so that he does not propagate and threaten other humans. On the other hand, although diagnostic labeling can obscure symptoms and behaviors relevant to threat assessment professionals, it can also function as an efficient communicator of probable symptom clusters for mental health professionals and signify the likely prognosis, or clinical outcome, if psychiatric or psychological treatment can be applied to the subject of concern.

Psychosis and delusions have also been found to be positively correlated with lethality risk (death or serious injury) in contemporary attacks on Western European politicians (James et al., 2007; phi = 0.49). Delusional content has strongly influenced the motivation, and thus the behavioral pathway, toward historical attacks on members of the British Royal Family (James et al., 2008). Hoffmann et al. (in press) have found that the majority of the small universe of potentially lethal attackers of public figures in Germany (1968 to 2004) were psychotic at the time ($N = 9$). All but one of these attacks occurred since 1990 and were mostly directed at politicians. A related study concerning mass murderers also found that psychosis is significantly and positively correlated with a higher casualty rate (Meloy et al., 2004a). However, in the ECSP study, Fein and Vossekuil (1999) found a significantly lower frequency of delusion ($p = .004$) between the attackers (25 percent) and the near-lethal approachers (60 percent) in their analysis ($n = 73$) of mental state at the time of the principal incident.

Moreover, the studies of attacks on public figures in the United States, the United Kingdom, and Western Europe discussed here underscore the fact that serious mental disorders do not mitigate the risk of a planned attack on a public figure. All of these studies indicate that despite the presence of mental illness, subjects can carefully plan an attack over the course of days, weeks, or months. What has not been studied is whether the nature of the mental disorder (e.g., a delusional belief in one's mission) may bring a *resolve and commitment* to the planning that would otherwise be absent, or at least marked by ambivalence, in the subject who was not delusional while planning an attack.

Predatory and Affective Violence

Most acts of violence toward public figures are predatory (instrumental)[2] and involve a weapon, most likely a firearm (de Becker et al., 2008; Meloy et al., 2004b). This was documented in the ECSP study and confirmed by the study of Western European attacks. In emerging research there is also a suggestion that most individuals who embarked on a pathway toward violence did not use mind-altering substances at the time of the attack. This is in stark contrast to affective violence,[3] in which substance abuse at the time of an attack is common (e.g., spousal violence, which is usually affective, commonly involves alcohol intoxication by the perpetrator, victim, or both; Miller, 1990).

It is a reasonable hypothesis, although untested, that subjects who engage in attack behavior toward a public figure *will not* use substances to increase the probability of tactical success, just as they typically will not explicitly threaten before an attack. There are a few cases, moreover, where subjects who engaged in predatory violence used psychotropic medications (barbiturates or sedatives/hypnotics) to deliberately main-

---

[2]This is a mode of violence that is planned, purposeful, emotionless, accompanied by low levels of autonomic arousal, and not preceded by an imminent threat (Meloy, 2006).

[3]This is a mode of violence that is impulsive, reactive, time limited, accompanied by emotion (anger and/or fear) and high levels of autonomic arousal, and preceded by a perceived imminent threat (Meloy, 2006).

tain a state of calmness during the violence. However, these cases did not involve attacks on public figures (Meloy and Mohandie, 2001). There is also the anecdotal finding in certain cases that specific loss (e.g., job, family, reputation, income) precedes an attack and may actually be the point at which the *date and time of the approach or attack is set*—even though an attack had been contemplated for weeks or months. This loss is either cumulative or sudden, and there is likely to be a *predisposition* to attack a public figure that precedes it but without specificity of time, target, or location. These patterns of loss have yet to be studied among attackers and assassins of public figures, particularly in relation to location, timing, and target selection.

Although the attack research indicates that most acts of violence toward public figures are predatory (planned, purposeful, emotionless) rather than affective (reactive, impulsive, emotional), the latter do occur. In one celebrity study (Meloy et al., 2008a), a majority of the small number of attacks ($n = 5$) against a sample of 159 celebrity stalking victims were affective and did not involve a weapon. They usually involved attempts to grab the celebrity or assault security personnel during a public appearance. This celebrity sample was embedded in the largest study of stalkers to date (Mohandie et al., 2006; $N = 1,005$). When all acts of violence ($n = 337$) were compared in this latter study, those stalkers who had an actual relationship (prior intimate or acquaintance groups) with the target were more likely to be affectively violent, and those without a relationship (public figure and private stranger groups) were more likely to be predatorily violent ($p = .001$). Affective violence toward a public figure appears most likely to occur when there is a perceived rejection by the public figure, which could happen in a moment, such as the public figure not shaking hands or making eye contact with the subject in a rope line or security personnel interfering with attempted contact between the subject and the public figure (James et al., 2010b). Clinically, this may be more likely in an individual who has a strong sense of entitled reciprocity and grandiosity.

Conflation of the Politics of Hatred

One of the most important emerging trends in threats toward public figures in the United States is *conflation* of the various politics of hatred, which then becomes a pathological fixation. This contemporary conflation usually includes hatred of African Americans, Jews, the federal government, abortion rights supporters, or gun control advocates. Pathological fixation strongly suggests the existence of a major mental disorder—or at least a paranoia-tinged rigid and intolerant belief system, which draws its content from the various politics of hatred. This conflation has a number of real-world stimuli: It is likely accelerated by the election of an African

American as president of the United States in November 2008, his initial appointment of a Jewish chief of staff characterized by the press as aggressive, a perceived expansion of the federal government through actions taken in response to the recession of 2008 to 2009, and President Obama's support of abortion rights.[4]

This conflation raises the question of whether there should be a strict operational demarcation between a terrorist threat and a fixated threat, especially if a fixated subject's secondary motivation is to instill public fear or foment revolution.[5] It also emphasizes the risk of an ideologically driven "lone terrorist" who acts outside of a terrorist cell or extremist group, often despite—or because of—failed attempts to associate with the latter (Puckitt, 2001; Biesterfeld and Meloy, 2008). Puckitt's finding that lone terrorists often unsuccessfully try to affiliate with an extremist group and are rejected (thus intensifying their bond to a radical ideology) has direct operational implications for surveillance of such groups. Timothy McVeigh and Terry Nichols attempted to associate with the Michigan Militia in the years prior to the Oklahoma City bombing in April 1995, but they were rejected by the group for advocating direct violence against the government (from author's files on *U.S. v. Timothy James McVeigh*).

What may at first appear to be a purely political motivation might actually mask a diagnosable psychiatric condition, wherein political, religious, or racial hatred provides the rationale for homicidal aggression.[6] Lance Corporal Kody Brittingham was arrested, along with two other Marines, in December 2008 for attempted armed robbery of a motel. In his barracks at Camp Lejeune, North Carolina, investigators found maps, photos, and personal vital statistics on then president-elect Barack Obama and white supremacist materials. There was also a letter titled "Operation Patriot":

---

[4]The irrationality of this acceleration in some quarters was evidenced by the substantial increase in firearms sales throughout the United States during the first six months of 2009, out of fear that President Obama would move to confiscate such weapons—despite the fact that the president had clearly expressed support for the individual rights' interpretation of the 2nd amendment, including the 2008 U.S. Supreme Court decision in *District of Columbia v. Heller*. *McDonald v. Chicago* further clarified these individual rights two years later (561 U.S. _____ 2010).

[5]Terrorism is defined by the Federal Bureau of Investigation as "the unlawful use of force or violence committed by a group or individual against persons or property to intimidate or coerce a government, the civilian population, or any segment thereof, in furtherance of political or social objectives" (Federal Bureau of Investigation, 1996).

[6]The clearest and most recent example of the completed assassination of a public figure that was politically motivated yet was interpreted in the subsequent criminal litigation as being primarily motivated by psychiatric disorder was the killing of Robert F. Kennedy by Sirhan Sirhan in 1968 (Meloy, 1992b).

I, Kody Brittingham, write this as a letter of intent. I'm in full mental health and clear judgment, having consciously made a decision, and in turn do so choose to carry out the actions entailed. I have sworn to defend my country, my Constitution, and the values and virtues of the aforementioned. My vow was to protect against all enemies, both foreign and domestic. I have found, through much research, evidence to support my current state of mind. Having found said domestic enemy (BHO), it is my duty and honor to carry out by all means necessary to protect my nation and her people from this threat. (Zeleny and Rutenberg, 2009)

Lance Corporal Brittingham pled guilty in August 2009 to threatening to kill the president and to attempted armed robbery. Although there is no publicly available evidence that he has a diagnosable mental disorder—again, the signs, symptoms, and behavior caused by any mental disorder are more important to threat assessment than the label—a conflation of racism and patriotism is a reasonable inference. Increased threat associated with the politics of hatred, at this time coming from the extreme right, has been documented in reports by the U.S. Department of Homeland Security (2009) and the Southern Poverty Law Center (2009).

Leakage

The warning behavior that is arguably the most important from an operational perspective is "leakage" of intent to harm a target, whether vague or specific, to third parties (O'Toole, 2000; Meloy and O'Toole, in press). Leakage is one of the seven types of warning behaviors noted earlier and is characteristic of both assassins of public figures and mass murderers (Hempel et al., 1999; Meloy et al., 2004a). Individuals in both groups want to carry out a very low frequency but highly catastrophic act of violence against an intended target (either identified beforehand or opportunistic). These are "black swan" events.[7]

In the ECSP study (Fein and Vossekuil, 1998, 1999), 63 percent of subjects ($N = 83$) had a history of indirect, conditional, or direct threats *about* their target, usually to family, friends, co-workers, or others known to the target. There were no direct threats to the target or law enforcement officials beforehand by those who attacked or assassinated their target. If near-lethal approachers are included, this direct threat frequency

---

[7]This term is borrowed from *The Black Swan* (Taleb, 2007) and refers to highly improbable events that have three characteristics: (1) they are outliers that most people would not consider possible; (2) they carry an extreme impact; and (3) we concoct explanations after the fact to make them seem predictable. One single observation can invalidate a general statement derived from years of confirmatory findings.

increases from 0 to 7 percent.[8] In the Western European study, 46 percent of attacks ($N = 24$) were preceded "by obvious and often flamboyant warning behaviors in the form of threatening or bizarre communications to politicians, public figures, or police forces" (James et al., 2007, p. 342). There were no cases in which the attack was preceded by a direct threat to kill the individual who was eventually attacked. Among adult mass murderers, the majority leak their intent to attack to third parties, but only a minority communicate a direct threat to their targets beforehand (Meloy et al., 2004a). Although the reasons for this dynamic likely vary from case to case, it is most plausible that the absence of a direct threat is motivated by a desire for tactical success. The prevalence of leakage is the inability of the subject to contain his or her excitement, satisfaction, or anxiety while researching, planning, and implementing an attack.

Leakage is also evident in journals, diaries, and electronically via the Internet. Online leaks have not yet been formally studied. A recent example of leakage on the Internet is the nine-month blogging carried out by George Sodini before committing mass murder near Pittsburgh, Pennsylvania, in August 2009. In his blog he discussed his intent, timing, preparations, and one "false start" but not an exact location. The irony of this case is that the entire world could have paid attention to him, but no one did.

New Threat Research

Although leakage is typically much more prevalent than a direct threat when investigating a problematic approacher or potential attacker of a public figure, new homicidal threat research, mostly related to stalking of nonpublic figures and in a mental health context, empirically supports the conventional belief that all threats should be taken seriously. Warren et al. (2007) found substantially higher rates of assault and even homicide in Australia following threats in 1993 and 1994 to kill among a large sample ($N = 613$) of subjects. The offense required that the threat produced fear in the victim. The individuals at highest risk for subsequent violence were young, had mental disorders, abused substances, and did not have prior criminal convictions. Among homicidal threateners, the rates of homicide and suicide almost exactly mirrored the results found in a classic study done more than 40 years ago (MacDonald, 1963) and were orders of magnitude higher than expected by chance (Warren et al., 2007).

---

[8]Lee Harvey Oswald did leave a threatening note with an FBI agent 10 days before the assassination of President John F. Kennedy, but it was a warning to the agent to leave his wife, Marina, alone and to stop harassing her. From 1961 to 1962 the U.S. Secret Service recorded 34 threats on the president's life from Texas (Bugliosi, 2007).

Within 10 years, 44 percent of the threateners were convicted of further violent offenses, including 3 percent ($n = 19$) for homicides. Twenty-six percent ($n = 5$) of the homicide victims were those originally threatened by the subject. Sixteen threateners (2.6 percent) committed suicide, and three were murdered. Substance abuse, prior violence, limited education, and untreated mental disorder contributed to any risk of violence by those who threatened to kill.

In another study (Smith, 2008), a sample of FBI threateners ($N = 96$) were more likely to act harmfully if their communications showed lower ambivalent hostility and higher conceptual complexity. Lower ambivalent hostility was related to a lack of paranoia; higher conceptual complexity was related to deliberative thinking. This finding of a lack of paranoia among those who harmed is consistent with the British Royal Family problematic approach studies discussed earlier, which found paranoia negatively associated with breach activity. Likewise, the ECSP and European attacks studies documented the minor role of paranoia among assassins, attackers, and near-lethal approachers. In the FBI study the author believed that the results could be generalized to all written threat cases of the FBI's National Center for the Analysis of Violent Crimes, although only 10 percent of the cases involved public figures as targets (Smith, 2008). Data continue to emerge to indicate that threatening communicators, if they are subsequently violent, might not attack the original target of the communicated threat.

Depression and Suicidality

Emerging research suggests the importance of *depression* and *suicidality* in the clinical motivation for an approach toward or attack of a public figure. Meloy et al. (2004b) found that many subjects evidenced a downward spiral in their lives in the months or year preceding the approach or attack, usually a combination of social failure and personal vulnerability to chronic anger, depression, or psychosis. Fein and Vossekuil (1998, 1999) found that 44 percent of subjects had a history of serious depression or despair and 24 percent had a history of suicidal attempts. James et al. (2007) found that 12 percent of Western European attackers clearly intended to die during the assault. Mohandie et al. (2006) found in their large study of stalkers that 25 percent evidenced suicidality (e.g., threats, gestures, attempts) in their histories. Perpetration of violence by persons with major mental disorder is correlated with adverse outcomes such as suicide and self-harm (Nicholls et al., 2006). As Douglas et al. (2009) wrote, "Negative symptoms that result in depression or suicidality may increase violence risk, as morbid thoughts of self-harm may change or expand in focus to include others" (p. 4).

Attacks on a public figure, depression, and suicidality appear to be linked for several reasons:

- the wish to "suicide by cop" (Mohandie et al., 2009) while attempting to attack or assassinate is a more public forum for ending one's life and may satisfy other narcissistic needs for attention;
- the "suicidal" communication beforehand may be one aspect of "final act" behavior;
- suicidal intent as one of several motivations for an attack on a public figure may be *positively correlated* with the amount of "lethal force" security surrounding the target; and
- suicidal desires or intent can be given a positive valence by redefining them as motivations for martyrdom and linking them to a religious or political cause (Menninger, 1938; Reik, 1941).

These motivations are, in turn, usually fueled by hatred of a particular race, ethnic group, religion, or political position, often combined with a fear of conspiracy or persecution by the targeted individual or group. Such fear may be paranoid, without any basis in reality, or it can be historically factual and reasonable given personal or group suffering at the hands of another.

Psychopathy

At the other end of the clinical spectrum, and typically devoid of depressive symptoms, is the psychopathic attacker or assassin. The construct of *psychopathy* has received virtually no attention in the research on stalking, threatening, and attacking public figures. Psychopathy, or psychopathic personality, is characterized by affective deficiency (i.e., absence of empathy, bonding, guilt, or remorse) and chronic antisocial behavior (criminal and noncriminal exploitation of others; Hare, 2003). Psychopathy has never been measured in either problematic approachers or attackers of public figures, although it has been theoretically proposed as an important construct (O'Toole et al., 2008). Most importantly, psychopathy accounts for the largest proportion of explainable variance in research on the risk of both criminal and civil violence (Monahan et al., 2001). It is a reliable and valid scientific construct that is relatively easily measured by trained professionals (Hare, 2003); it correlates with the risk of predatory (i.e., planned, purposeful) violence, which is the most likely mode of violence when a public figure is attacked (Meloy et al., 2008b); and there now exists a security and law enforcement assessment tool for measuring psychopathy (P-SCAN, available from http://www.mhs.com).

The relationship between psychopathy and psychosis is also notable.

When they coexist in a violent subject, the former will typically play a much larger role than the latter in accounting for the violence. The effect of psychosis on violence risk indicates a small, though reliable, effect size of $r = .12$ to $.16$ (Douglas et al., 2009).[9] Psychopathy and its impact on violence show effect sizes between .25 and .30 (Douglas et al., 2009). In general, psychosis shows a significantly lower odds ratio for the prediction of violence than personality disorder.

The relevance to attacks on public figures is the operational importance, though not yet measured, of psychopathy in particular and personality disorder in general in motivating a near-lethal approach, attack, or assassination. In the ECSP study (Fein and Vossekuil, 1998, 1999), 39 percent of the subjects were never evaluated by a mental health professional, and 57 percent had no history of delusional ideas. Seventy-five percent of attackers were not delusional during the principal incident, and 40 percent of near-lethal approachers were not delusional. In the European attacks study (James et al., 2007), 46 percent were determined to have no mental disorder, highlighting the reliable absence of mental disorder in a proportion of public figure attackers and the likely presence, though unmeasured, of character pathology (such as psychopathy) as a motivation for the assault.

Clarke (1982) identified Type III subjects in his typology of U.S. assassins as psychopaths, who experience life as meaningless, and the motivation to assassinate is the nonpolitical expression of rage in someone devoid of human attachments who does not experience the more socialized emotions of guilt, shame, or remorse. As he wrote, "They are belligerently contemptuous of morality and social convention" (1982, p. 15). He identified three American assassins who fit this third type: (1) Guiseppe Zangara, an Italian immigrant who attempted to kill President Franklin Roosevelt on February 13, 1933; (2) Arthur Bremer,[10] who shot and crippled Alabama Governor George Wallace on May 15, 1972; and (3) John Hinckley, Jr., who shot and wounded President Ronald Reagan on March 30, 1981. Again, empirical measurement of psychopathy in these individuals has not been done, but given the extensive published materials on these subjects, it could be accomplished without a clinical interview by using a standardized observational instrument, the Psychopathy Checklist–Revised (Hare, 2003).

---

[9]The addition of substance abuse produces a substantially larger effect size than does psychosis alone ($d = .97$; Douglas et al., 2009).

[10]Bremer was released from a Maryland prison in November 2007. He is the first assassin to ever be released from custody in the United States. During his 35 years in prison, he refused all mental health assessment and treatment.

Pathway to Violence

Emerging research confirms the existence of a *pathway to violence* (Calhoun and Weston, 2003)—consisting of the stages of grievance, ideation, research/planning, preparation, breach, and attack—but it is more complex than first formulated. Most approaches to a public figure are not intended to be or are predictive of violence (Meloy et al., 2008b). A pathway to violence depends on the motivation for communication and approach and the *perceived* reaction of the public figure, which will virtually always be personalized by the subject. For example, a subject whose initial approach is motivated by a desire for help might subsequently become aggressive and hostile if the expected response is not forthcoming. Likewise, there may be no pathway at all, other than an initial approach resulting in a successful breach of security and an attack. An example is the assassination of Swedish Foreign Minister Anna Lindh on September 10, 2003. Her attacker, Mijailo Mijailovic, had a fantasy of killing someone famous and actually reported to a psychiatric clinic that he had murdered someone six days before the Lindh assassination. He was diagnosed with "a personality disorder intermittently bordering on psychosis" and prescribed medications. He then subsequently and accidentally encountered Ms. Lindh, who was without a security detail, in a Stockholm department store. Minutes later he stabbed her to death in front of her friend. She was a target of opportunity, and a thorough investigation indicated no evidence of prior planning (Unsgaard and Meloy, 2011).

Besides a pathway to violence, there are other domains of risk. A subject might disrupt the public figure's schedule, there may be recidivism or persistence of pursuit (James et al., 2009b), or a problematic approacher might embarrass or inconvenience a public figure target through behaviors that pose no physical threat.

Communicated Threats Schematic

A schematic has been proposed to improve the analytic clarity of communicated threats; it includes motivation, means, manner, and material content (Meloy et al., 2008b). *Motivation* refers to whether the threat is expressive (to regulate affect of the threatener) or instrumental (to control the behavior of the target). *Means* refers to the method of communication, such as letters, e-mails, telephone calls, text messages, and faxes. *Manner* refers to whether the threat is communicated directly or indirectly to the target. *Material content* refers to all material aspects of the threat itself, usually analyzable through the use of forensic technology, such as linguistics, DNA transfer evidence, fingerprint evidence, or graphic presentation. This face-valid schematic has not yet been tested for any predictive or concurrent validity but is an attempt to clarify terms used to study communications that are not mutually exclusive (e.g., conditional threat, veiled threat, direct threat) and have been inconsistently defined in previous studies.

Children of Public Figures

Another concern—inordinate interest in the children of a public figure—also deserves attention from a problematic approach or threat perspective. Inappropriate communication (frequent, long-duration, bizarre, or odd) to the minor children of famous people usually arises from three psychological sources: (1) nonpsychotic transference, or the shifting of emotions from one's own children, or oneself as a child, or the absence of children, to the offspring of a public figure; (2) psychotic transference, or a delusional belief that the subject is related to or has an important role in the children's actual lives; and (3) pedophilic interest—an almost exclusively male subject's interest in minors as sexual objects. There is no published research on this topic concerning the children of public figures, although there are many safety programs in place in schools and elsewhere for all children who may encounter a relative or stranger with malevolent intent. There is at least one private study that has been completed related to crimes against children of public figures, but the findings of the study are unavailable.

The absence until 2009 of two prepubescent children in the White House since the presidency of John F. Kennedy warrants careful and immediate study of these potential concerns and threats. Perhaps the most onerous threat toward the children of public figures is kidnapping. Although research in this area is dated and no published research has focused exclusively on the children of public figures, there were 115 stereotypical kidnappings in 1999, defined as abductions perpetrated by a stranger or slight acquaintance and involving a child who was transported 50 or more miles, detained overnight, held for ransom or with the intent to keep the child permanently, or killed. In 40 percent of these cases the child was killed, and in another 4 percent the child was not recovered. Two-thirds of these stereotypical kidnappings involved female victims between the ages of 6 and 14 (Finkelhor et al., 2002). Other studies involving large national samples have found that offender and offense characteristics in child abductions vary significantly according to the victim's age, gender, and race (Boudreaux et al., 1999). For example, sexual gratification is the most likely motivation for stranger abduction of a girl 5 to 10 years old. Time and distance intervals are also critical to case solvability in child abduction murders (Brown and Keppel, 2007). Most child abductions, though, are perpetrated by family members or close relatives (Boudreaux et al., 1999).

FUTURE OPERATIONAL RESEARCH

The map is not the territory. In other words, despite a theory's elegance or the comprehensiveness of data collection, research results will not exactly reflect reality. There will always be known unknowns, unknown unknowns, and individual differences that are not captured by large-group research, which is the cornerstone of the social and behavioral sciences. On rare occasions, "black swans"—events that are completely unpredictable yet catastrophic—will appear (Taleb, 2007), challenging historical beliefs and assumptions that have guided operational decisions, even when based on a robust research program.

Research studies of individuals who problematically approach, escalate, and in a few cases attack public figures should not only utilize nomothetic (large-group) data randomly drawn from recent case management files but also focus on select cases and the individual differences defining them. Subjects of particular interest to law enforcement, security, and intelligence agencies because of their unusual or outlier behaviors could yield important data by being forensically evaluated with standardized tests and measures if possible.[11] Sensitivity to all forms of methodological challenges in research (including study design, measurement, and confounding factors) should be rigorously maintained to minimize their impact on findings and, when unavoidable, should be set forth as limitations.

The study of those who approach or attack public figures is a nascent science, but it can bring an operational efficiency to those tasked with protecting public figures. Research continues to refine our understanding of the interplay of protective intelligence gathering and personal protection and contributes to minimizing the vulnerability of public figures to an attack. The danger in many cases is quite real. As Hoffmann and Meloy (2008, p. 191) have written, "Disappointment or humiliation is the very predictable outcome when a public figure is pursued. The idolized figure is now beneath contempt. Yearning becomes disgust. Love may even become hatred. Rationalizations are put into place. Delusion may bring a resolve that is immutable. Aggression intensifies. Revenge is in the air."

---

[11]Such testing would typically include standardized measures of IQ (WAIS IV), personality and psychopathology measures (Rorschach, MMPI-2, PAI), neuropsychological screening instruments, and other measures as needed (malingering, memory, etc.). Such measures allow for the comparison of a particular subject to large clinical and normative samples and therefore enhance the evaluator's ability to accurately measure both normality and abnormality.

REFERENCES

Biesterfeld, J., and J.R. Meloy. 2008. The public figure assassin as terrorist. In J.R., Meloy, L. Sheridan, and J. Hoffmann, eds., *Stalking, Threatening, and Attacking Public Figures: A Psychological and Behavioral Analysis* (pp. 143-162). New York: Oxford University Press.

Boudreaux, M., W. Lord, and R. Dutra. 1999. Child abduction: Age-based analysis of offender, victim, and offense characteristics in 550 cases of alleged child disappearance. *Journal of Forensic Sciences*, 44:539-550.

Brown, K., and R. Keppel. 2007. Child abduction murder: An analysis of the effect of time and distance separation between murder incident sites and solvability. *Journal of Forensic Sciences*, 52(1):137-145.

Bugliosi, V. 2007. *Reclaiming History: The Assassination of President John F. Kennedy.* New York: W.W. Norton.

Calhoun, F. 1998. *Hunters and Howlers: Threats Against Federal Judicial Officials in the United States, 1789-1993.* Arlington, VA: U.S. Department of Justice, U.S. Marshals Service.

Calhoun, F., and S. Weston. 2003. *Contemporary Threat Management: A Practical Guide for Identifying, Assessing, and Managing Individuals of Violent Intent.* San Diego, CA: Specialized Training Services.

Calhoun, F., and S. Weston. 2008. On public figure howlers. In J.R. Meloy, L. Sheridan, and J. Hoffmann, eds., *Stalking, Threatening, and Attacking Public Figures: A Psychological and Behavioral Analysis* (pp. 105-122). New York: Oxford University Press.

Clarke, J. 1982. *American Assassins.* Princeton, NJ: Princeton University Press.

De Becker, G., T. Taylor, and J. Marquart. 2008. *Just 2 Seconds: Using Time and Space to Defeat Assassins.* Studio City, CA: Gavin de Becker Center for the Study and Reduction of Violence.

Dietz, P. 1986. Mass, serial, and sensational homicides. *Bulletin of the New York Academy of Medicine*, 62(5):477-491.

Dietz, P., and D. Martell. 1989. *Mentally Disordered Offenders in Pursuit of Celebrities and Politicians.* Washington, DC: National Institute of Justice.

Dietz, P., D. Matthews, C. Van Duyne, D. Martell, C. Perry, T. Stewart, and J. Warren. 1991a. Threatening and otherwise inappropriate letters to Hollywood celebrities. *Journal of Forensic Sciences*, 36:185-209.

Dietz, P., D. Matthews, D. Martell, T. Stewart, D. Hrouda, and J. Warren. 1991b. Threatening and otherwise inappropriate letters to members of the United States Congress. *Journal of Forensic Sciences*, 36:1445-1468.

Douglas, K., L. Guy, and S. Hart. 2009. Psychosis as a risk factor for violence to others: A meta-analysis. *Psychological Bulletin*, 135(5):679-706.

Federal Bureau of Investigation. 1996. *Terrorism in the United States.* Washington, DC: Counterterrorism Threat Assessment and Warning Unit, National Security Division, Federal Bureau of Investigation.

Fein, R., and B. Vossekuil. 1998. Preventing attacks on public officials and public figures: A Secret Service perspective. In J.R. Meloy, ed., *The Psychology of Stalking: Clinical and Forensic Perspectives* (pp.176-194). San Diego, CA: Academic Press.

Fein, R., and B. Vossekuil. 1999. Assassination in the United States: An operational study of recent assassins, attackers, and near-lethal approachers. *Journal of Forensic Sciences*, 44(2):321-333.

Fein, R., B. Vossekuil, and G. Holden. 1995. *Threat Assessment: An Approach to Prevent Targeted Violence.* Washington, DC: Office of Justice Programs, National Institute of Justice, U.S. Department of Justice.

Finkelhor, D., H. Hammer, and A. Sedlak. 2002. *Nonfamily Abducted Children: National Estimates and Characteristics.* Washington, DC: Office of Juvenile Justice and Delinquency Prevention, Office of Justice Programs, U.S. Department of Justice.

Hare, R.D. 2003. *Manual for the Psychopathy—Checklist Revised, 2nd edition.* Toronto, Canada: Multihealth Systems.

Hart, S., C. Michie, and D. Cooke. 2007. Precision of actuarial risk assessment instruments: Evaluating the "margin of error" of group v. individual predictions of violence. *British Journal of Psychiatry,* 190(Suppl. 49):S60-S65.

Hempel, A., J.R. Meloy, and T. Richards. 1999. Offender and offense characteristics of a nonrandom sample of mass murderers. *Journal of the American Academy of Psychiatry and the Law,* 27(2):213-225.

Hoffmann, J., and J.R. Meloy. 2008. Contributions from attachment theory and psychoanalysis to advance understanding of public figure stalking and attacking. In J.R. Meloy, L. Sheridan, and J. Hoffmann, eds., *Stalking, Threatening, and Attacking Public Figures* (pp. 165-194). New York: Oxford University Press.

Hoffmann, J., J.R. Meloy, A. Guldimann, and A. Ermer. In press. Public figure attacks in Germany, 1968-2004. *Behavioral Sciences and the Law.*

James, D.V., P. Mullen, J.R. Meloy, M. Pathe, F. Farnham, L. Preston, and B. Darnley. 2007. The role of mental disorder in attacks on European politicians, 1990-2004. *Acta Psychiatrica Scandinavica,* 116(5):334-344.

James, D.V., P. Mullen, M. Pathé, J.R. Meloy, F. Farnham, L. Preston, and B. Darnley. 2008. Attacks on the British Royal Family: The role of psychotic illness. *Journal of the American Academy of Psychiatry and the Law,* 36:59-67.

James, D.V., J.R. Meloy, P. Mullen, M. Pathé, F. Farnham, L. Preston, and B. Darnley. 2010a. Abnormal attentions toward the British Royal Family: Factors associated with approach and escalation. *Journal of the American Academy of Psychiatry and the Law,* 38(3):329-340.

James, D.V., P. Mullen, J.R. Meloy, M. Pathé, L. Preston, B. Darnley, F. Farnham, and M. Scalora. 2010b. Stalkers and harassers of British Royalty: An exploration of proxy behaviors for violence. *Behavioral Sciences and the Law,* doi: 10.1002/bsl.922.

James, D.V., P.E. Mullen, M. Pathé, J.R. Meloy, L.F. Preston, B. Darnley, and F. Farnham. 2009a. Stalkers and harassers of royalty: The role of mental illness and motivation. *Psychological Medicine,* 39(9):1479-1490.

James, D.V., T. McEwan, R. MacKenzie, J.R. Meloy, P. Mullen, M. Pathé, F. Farnham, L. Preston, and B. Darnley. 2009b. Persistence in stalking: A comparison of general and public figure stalking samples. *Journal of Forensic Psychiatry and Psychology,* 21(2):283-305.

Junginger, J. 1996. Psychosis and violence: The case for a content analysis of psychotic experience. *Schizophrenia Bulletin,* 22(1):91-103.

Knoll, J. 2010. The "pseudocommando" mass murderer: Part I, The psychology of revenge and obliteration. *Journal of the American Academy of Psychiatry and the Law,* 38(1):87-94.

Leets, L., G. De Becker, and H. Giles. 1995. Fans: Exploring expressed motivations for contacting celebrities. *Journal of Language and Social Psychology,* 14(1-2):102-123.

MacDonald, J.M. 1963. The threat to kill. *American Journal of Psychiatry,* 120:125-130.

MacKenzie, R., T. McEwan, M. Pathe, D. James, J. Ogloff, and P. Mullen. 2009. *The Stalking Risk Profile: Guidelines for the Assessment and Management of Stalkers.* Melbourne, Australia: Centre for Forensic Behavioural Science, Monash University.

Mailer, N. 1995. *Oswald's Tale: An American Mystery.* New York: Random House.

Meloy, J.R. 1992a. *Violent Attachments.* Northvale, NJ: Aronson.

Meloy, J.R. 1992b. Revisiting the Rorschach of Sirhan Sirhan. *Journal of Personality Assessment,* 58(3):548-570.

Meloy, J.R., ed. 1998. *The Psychology of Stalking: Clinical and Forensic Perspectives.* San Diego, CA: Academic Press.

Meloy, J.R. 2006. The empirical basis and forensic application of affective and predatory violence. *Australian and New Zealand Journal of Psychiatry,* 40(6-7):539-547.

Meloy, J.R., J. Hoffmann, A. Guldimann and D. James. Unpublished. The concept of warning behaviors in threat assessment. Available: http://www.forensis.org [accessed June 2010].

Meloy, J.R., A. Hempel, T. Gray, K. Mohandie, A. Shiva, and T. Richards. 2004a. A comparative analysis of North American adolescent and adult mass murderers. *Behavioral Sciences and the Law*, 22(3):291-309.

Meloy, J.R., D.V. James, P.E. Mullen, M. Pathé, F. Farnham, L. Preston, and B. Darnley. 2004b. A research review of public figure threats, approaches, attacks, and assassinations in the United States. *Journal of Forensic Sciences*, 49(5):1086-1093.

Meloy, J.R., D.V. James, P.E. Mullen, M. Pathé, F. Farnham, L. Preston, and B. Darnley. 2010. Factors associated with escalation and problematic approaches toward public figures. *Journal of Forensic Sciences*, doi: 10.1111/j.1556-4029.2010.01574.x.

Meloy, J.R., and K. Mohandie. 2001. Investigating the role of screen violence in specific homicide cases. *Journal of Forensic Sciences*, 46(5):1113-1118.

Meloy, J.R., K. Mohandie, and M. Green. 2008a. A forensic investigation of those who stalk celebrities. In J.R. Meloy, L. Sheridan, and J. Hoffmann, eds., *Stalking, Threatening, and Attacking Public Figures: A Psychological and Behavioral Analysis* (pp. 37-54). New York: Oxford University Press.

Meloy, J.R., and M.E. O'Toole. In press. The concept of leakage in threat assessment. *Behavioral Sciences and the Law*.

Meloy, J.R., L. Sheridan, and J. Hoffmann, eds. 2008b. *Stalking, Threatening, and Attacking Public Figures: A Psychological and Behavioral Analysis*. New York: Oxford University Press.

Menninger, K. 1938. *Man Against Himself*. New York: Harcourt Brace.

Miller, B. 1990. The interrelationships between alcohol, drugs and family violence. In M. De la Rosa, E. Lambert, and B. Gropper, eds., *Drugs and Violence: Causes, Correlates, and Consequences* (pp. 186-216). Washington, DC: National Institutes of Health, U.S. Department of Health and Human Services.

Mohandie, K., J.R. Meloy, M. McGowan, and J. Williams. 2006. The RECON typology of stalking: Reliability and validity based upon a large sample of North American stalkers. *Journal of Forensic Sciences*, 51(1):147-155.

Mohandie, K., J.R. Meloy, and P. Collins. 2009. Suicide by cop among officer-involved shooting cases. *Journal of Forensic Sciences*, 54(2):1-7.

Monahan, J. 2000. Clinical and actuarial predictions of violence. In D. Faigman, D. Kaye, M. Saks, and J. Sanders, eds., *Modern Scientific Evidence: The Law and Science of Expert Testimony* (pp. 300-318). St. Paul, MN: West Publishing.

Monahan, J. 2010. Classification of violence risk. In R. Otto and K. Douglas, eds., *Handbook of Violence Risk Assessment* (pp. 187-198). New York: Routledge.

Monahan, J., H. Steadman, E. Silver, P. Appelbaum, P. Robbins, E. Mulvey, L. Roth, T. Grisso, and S. Banks. 2001. *Rethinking Risk Assessment: The MacArthur Study of Mental Disorder and Violence*. New York: Oxford University Press.

Mullen, P., D. James, J.R. Meloy, M. Pathé, F. Farnham, L. Preston, B. Darnley, and J. Berman. 2009a. The fixated and the pursuit of public figures. *Journal of Forensic Psychiatry and Psychology*, 20(1):33-47.

Mullen, P., M. Pathé, and R. Purcell. 2009b. *Stalkers and Their Victims, 2nd edition*. London, UK: Cambridge University Press.

Nicholls, T., J. Brink, S. Desmarais, C. Webster, and M. Martin. 2006. The Short-Term Assessment of Risk and Treatability (START): A prospective validation study in a forensic psychiatric sample. *Assessment*, 13(3):313-327.

O'Toole, M.E. 2000. *The School Shooter: A Threat Assessment Perspective*. Quantico, VA: Critical Incident Response Group, FBI Academy, National Center for the Analysis of Violent Crime.

O'Toole, M.E., S. Smith, and R.D. Hare. 2008. Psychopathy and predatory stalking of public figures. In J.R. Meloy, L. Sheridan, and J. Hoffmann, eds., *Stalking, Threatening, and Attacking Public Figures: A Psychological and Behavioral Analysis* (pp. 215-243). New York: Oxford University Press.

Phillips, R.T. 2006. Assessing presidential stalkers and assassins. *Journal of the American Academy of Psychiatry and the Law*, 34(2):154-164.

Phillips, R.T. 2008. Psychiatric consultation to the United States Secret Service. In J.R. Meloy, L. Sheridan, and J. Hoffmann, eds., *Stalking, Threatening, and Attacking Public Figures: A Psychological and Behavioral Analysis* (pp. 363-385). New York: Oxford University Press.

Puckitt, K.M. 2001. *The Lone Terrorist: The Search for Connection and Its Relationship to Societal-Level Violence*. Washington, DC: Counterterrorism Division, Federal Bureau of Investigation, U.S. Department of Justice.

Reik, T. 1941. *Masochism in Modern Man.* New York: Farrar Straus.

Rothstein, A. 1980. *The Narcissistic Pursuit of Perfection*. New York: International Universities Press.

Scalora, M.J., J.V. Baumgartner, D. Callaway, W. Zimmerman, M.A. Hatch-Maillette, C.N. Covell, R.E. Palarea, J.A. Krebs, and D.O. Washington. 2002a. An epidemiological assessment of problematic contacts to members of Congress. *Journal of Forensic Sciences*, 47(6):1360-1364.

Scalora, M.J., J.V. Baumgartner, D. Callaway, W. Zimmerman, M.A. Hatch-Maillette, C.N. Covell, R.E. Palarea, J.A. Krebs, and D.O. Washington. 2002b. Risk factors for approach behavior toward the U.S. Congress. *Journal of Threat Assessment*, 2(2):35-55.

Scalora, M.J., J. Baumgartner, and G. Plank. 2003. The relationship of mental illness to targeted contact behavior toward state government agencies and officials. *Behavioral Sciences and the Law*, 21(2):239-249.

Schlesinger, L. 2006. Celebrity stalking, homicide, and suicide: A psychological autopsy. *International Journal of Offender Therapy and Comparative Criminology*, 50(1):39-46.

Schoeneman-Morris, K., M.J. Scalora, G. Chang, W. Zimmerman, and Y. Garner. 2007. A comparison of email versus letter threat contacts toward members of the United States Congress. *Journal of Forensic Sciences*, 52(5):1142-1147.

Smith, S. 2008. From violent words to violent deeds: Assessing risk from FBI threatening communication cases. In J.R. Meloy, L. Sheridan, and J. Hoffmann, eds., *Stalking, Threatening, and Attacking Public Figures: A Psychological and Behavioral Analysis* (pp. 435-455). New York: Oxford University Press.

Southern Poverty Law Center. 2009. *The Second Wave: Return of the Militias*. Montgomery, AL: Southern Poverty Law Center.

Taleb, N. 2007. *The Black Swan*. New York: Random House.

Unsgaard, E., and J.R. Meloy. 2011. The assassination of the Swedish Minister for Foreign Affairs. *Journal of Forensic Sciences*. Available: http://onlinelibrary.Wiley.com/doi/10.1111/j.1556-4029.2010.01653.x/full [accessed January 2011].

U.S. Department of Homeland Security. 2009. *Rightwing Extremism: Current Economic and Political Climate Fueling Resurgence in Radicalization and Recruitment*. Washington, DC: Office of Intelligence and Analysis, U.S. Department of Homeland Security.

Warren, L., P. Mullen, S. Thomas, J. Ogloff, and P. Burgess. 2007. Threats to kill: A follow-up study. *Psychological Medicine*, 38(4):599-605.

Zeleny, J., and J. Rutenberg. 2009. Threats against Obama spiked early. *The New York Times*, May 19, p. A1.

Appendix

Biographical Sketches of Contributors

Daniel Rex Bernard is a doctoral student in the Department of Communication, a graduate research assistant in the Department of Communication, and a research associate for the Center for Risk and Crisis Management, all at the University of Oklahoma. His areas of research include the development of technology in theoretical and applied communication studies, risk and crisis communication, deception detection, and social influence and the development of persuasive campaigns. He holds an M.A. in communication from California State University at Fresno.

Cherie Chauvin, *Editor,* is a program officer at the National Research Council, working on several studies and workshops relevant to defense and national security issues. Previously, she held several positions with the U.S. Department of Defense's Defense Intelligence Agency (DIA), where her work included support for military operations and liaison relationships in Japan, South Korea, and Mongolia, as well as conducting intelligence collection operations in Afghanistan to answer strategic and tactical military intelligence requirements. In recognition of her service, she was awarded the DIA Civilian Expeditionary Medal, the Department of the Army Commander's Award for Civilian Service, and the Office of the Director of National Intelligence National Meritorious Unit Citation. She holds a B.S. in cognitive science from the University of California at San Diego, an M.A. in international relations from the Maxwell School at Syracuse University, and an M.S. in strategic intelligence from the National Defense Intelligence College.

Cindy K. Chung is a consultant and senior investigator for various text analysis projects in health psychology, personality psychology, and the counterintelligence field and a postdoctoral fellow at the University of Texas at Austin. She has been involved in the development of text analysis tools and methods across several languages. Her work on psychological assessments based on natural language has been published in multiple journal articles and book chapters. She holds a Ph.D. in social and personality psychology from the University of Texas at Austin.

J. Reid Meloy is a clinical professor of psychiatry at the School of Medicine of the University of California at San Diego, an adjunct professor at the University of San Diego School of Law, and a faculty member of the San Diego Psychoanalytic Institute. He is also a consultant to the counterintelligence division of the FBI, a member of the Fixated Research Group for the United Kingdom's Home Office concerning threats to the Royal Family and British political figures, and a teacher for the Netherlands National Police. He has also been a technical consultant to the television program CSI since its inception in 2001. He is a fellow of the American Academy of Forensic Sciences, past president of the American Academy of Forensic Psychology, and president of Forensis, Inc., a nonprofit, public benefit corporation devoted to forensic psychiatric and psychological research. He has authored, coauthored, or edited more than 200 papers and 10 books. He holds a diploma in forensic psychology of the American Board of Professional Psychology.

H. Dan O'Hair is dean of the College of Communications and Information Studies and professor of communication at the University of Kentucky. He has published more than 90 articles and chapters and 15 books on risk and health communication, public relations, business communication, media management, communication, risk management, and terrorism. He has served on the editorial boards of numerous research journals and is a past editor of the *Journal of Applied Communication Research*. He is a past president of the National Communication Association, and he has served as an education and training consultant to dozens of private, nonprofit, and government organizations. He holds a Ph.D. in communication from the University of Oklahoma.

James W. Pennebaker is professor and chair of the Department of Psychology and the Regents Centennial Professor of Liberal Arts at the University of Texas at Austin. His research explores the links among natural language, traumatic experience, and health at the individual, group, and cultural levels. His earlier research focused on how writing or talking about emotional upheavals influences mental and physical health. More recently, in collaboration with colleagues in computational linguistics, cognitive psychology, communication, and social psychology, he has been examining how people's natural use of words can be powerful predictors of people's health, personality, social situations, and the ways they relate to others. He received the Pavlov Award from the Pavlovian Society. He is the author or editor of 8 books and more than 200 articles. He holds a Ph.D. from the University of Texas at Austin and an honorary doctorate from the Catholic University of Louvain-la-Neuve.

Randy R. Roper is a doctoral student in the Communication Department at the University of Oklahoma. His areas of research include interpersonal and organizational communication, with an emphasis on family conflict and grief communication. He holds a B.S. in public relations and an M.A. in family life ministry from Oklahoma Christian University.

Philip E. Rubin is chief executive officer and a senior scientist at Haskins Laboratories in New Haven, Connecticut, a research institute with a primary focus on the science of the spoken and written word and their biological basis. He is also an adjunct professor in the Department of Surgery, Otolaryngology, a research affiliate in the Department of Psychology, and a fellow of Trumbull College, all at Yale University. Previously, he was the director of the Division of Behavioral and Cognitive Sciences at the National Science Foundation. He has served as cochair of the interagency Committee on Science Human Subjects Research Subcommittee of the National Science and Technology Council (NSTC), under the auspices of the Executive Office of the President and a member of the NSTC Interagency Working Group on Social, Behavioral and Economic Sciences Task Force on Anti-Terrorism Research and Development. He is the chair of the Board on Behavioral, Cognitive, and Sensory Sciences of the National Research Council. He received a B.A. from Brandeis University in psychology and linguistics and an M.A. and a Ph.D. from the University of Connecticut in experimental psychology.

Barbara A. Wanchisen is director of the Board on Behavioral, Cognitive, and Sensory Sciences and the Board on Human-Systems Integration of the National Research Council. Previously, she was the executive director of the Federation of Behavioral, Psychological, and Cognitive Sciences, and she was instrumental in the founding of the federation's Foundation for the Advancement of Behavioral and Brain Sciences to assume the educational mission of the federation. Prior to her Washington work, she was a professor in the Department of Psychology and director of the college-wide Honors Program at Baldwin-Wallace College. She is a member of the Psychonomic Society, the Association for Behavior Analysis-International, and the American Association for the Advancement of Science and a fellow of the American Psychological Association. She has served on the editorial boards of the *Journal of the Experimental Analysis of Behavior* and *The Behavior Analyst*. She received a B.A. in English and philosophy from Bloomsburg University, an M.A. in English from Villanova University, and a Ph.D. in experimental psychology from Temple University.